# THE sew simple
## GUIDE TO EASY SEWING AND EMBELLISHING

editors of NEWS

Create with Confidence

D1308528

The *Sew Simple* Guide to Easy Sewing and Embellishing
© 2012 by the Editors of *Sew News* Magazine

sewNEWS

Martingale®
19021 120th Ave. NE, Suite 102
Bothell, WA 98011 USA
ShopMartingale.com

*Sew News,* ISSN 0273-8120, is published bimonthly by Creative Crafts Group, LLC, 741 Corporate Circle, Suite A, Golden, CO 80401, www.sewnews.com.

Printed in China
17 16 15 14 13 12        8 7 6 5 4 3 2 1

**Library of Congress Cataloging-in-Publication Data is available upon request.**

ISBN: 978-1-60468-165-9

## Mission Statement

Dedicated to providing quality products and service to inspire creativity.

## Credits

President & CEO • Tom Wierzbicki

Editor in Chief • Mary V. Green

Design Director • Paula Schlosser

Managing Editor • Karen Costello Soltys

Technical Editor • Rebecca Kemp Brent

Copy Editor • Marcy Heffernan

Production Manager • Regina Girard

Text & Cover Designer • Shelly Garrison

Illustrators • Laure Noe, Joyce Robinson, Aaron Ishaeik, Cherished Solutions, Katie Kolupke, Melinda Bylow, & Adrienne Smitke

Photographer • Joe Hancook Studio (Joe Hancook, Jon Rose, and Scott Wallace)

# CONTENTS

# INTRODUCTION

Yes, sewing *can* be simple.

It's hard to believe—especially when your thread breaks or bunches up beneath the fabric and all you want to do is throw in the towel—but sewing really can be a breeze. With a few quick-and-easy troubleshooting tips, you'll feel like a pro no matter how long you've been sewing. You'll be ready to tackle the most difficult sewing projects without batting an eye.

Maybe you've just purchased a machine and don't know where to begin. Maybe you haven't touched your machine in years and need a refresher course. Maybe you're an expert and want to teach others. Whatever the case may be, you'll enjoy having a basic reference guide to turn to when preparing, constructing, and finishing a sewing project.

One of the most important decisions when preparing for a sewing project is fabric choice. Many people choose fabric based on the color and pattern, but the feel of the fabric certainly comes into play. Plush fabric with a high pile is often a popular choice because it's so soft and cuddly. But once you start sewing it, the fabric often sheds, stretches, and is downright unruly. Leather is another popular choice because of its versatility and high-fashion allure. But stick an errant pin in the leather and you've got a hole for good. Before purchasing fabric, consult "Sewing with . . ." on page 65 to find the right fabric for your project and comfort level.

Pattern manufacturers often don't explain basic construction terms and techniques, making it difficult to decipher instructions. This frustration can cause a sewist to give up even before starting. After reading "Sewing Basics," you'll be familiar with the most common techniques, from cutting and marking to binding and buttonholes. Plus, added shortcuts and tips will make these tasks easier than ever before.

Finishing a project is the most gratifying part of the sewing process. But the most fun part is embellishing. Adding a little something such as hand embroidery, yarn couching, or metallic foiling makes the project unique and personal. Turn to "Build Your Embellishing Skills" on page 79 for seven embellishment options that will take your project from ordinary to extraordinary.

Keep this handy reference guide by your side to arm yourself with the information you need to complete each project you start. And when people marvel at your finished projects, remember that no one has to know just how easy they were to create!

Happy sewing,
Ellen March
*Sew News* Editor-in-Chief

# SEWING BASICS

# CUTTING

Accurately cutting out a pattern is as easy as following the lines. But since cutting is permanent, double-check your layout first to prevent mistakes.

To make cutting easier and more accurate, use fabric shears with long blades and a bent handle. These can be purchased for either left- or right-handed cutting. Keep them sharp and use them only for fabric; paper dulls scissors very quickly. Use long strokes for straight edges and shorter ones for curves.

If using a multisized pattern, double-check that you're cutting along the correct line. Trace over the line with a marker or pen if necessary, especially when using multiple sizes to create a custom fit.

Trace over the cutting line on multisized patterns to make cutting on the correct line a no-brainer.

You can use a rotary cutter and mat if you prefer. Make sure to keep the mat under the area being cut. Use a sharp blade and acrylic ruler as a guide for the most accurate results, although you can cut gentle curves without a ruler. For greater accuracy, use shears for cutting deeper curves or more difficult areas.

Don't use pinking shears to cut the fabric—pinking shears dull quickly and don't give an accurate edge to follow when sewing the seam. Instead, use the pinking shears to finish the fabric edges after the seam is sewn.

Cut with the fabric grain for best results. The grain direction is usually indicated on the pattern cutting line by a small scissors illustration. If the fabric has a pile or nap, cut with the nap. Don't lift the fabric as you cut because this may cause inaccuracies. Instead, lay one hand flat on the pattern and fabric while cutting with the other hand.

Cut around notches or cut off the notch and make a ⅛" slash into the seam allowance at the notch point. Take care with the latter method—don't cut too deeply, and don't use this method for fabrics that ravel or rip easily. Clipping into the seam allowances also leaves less fabric for any alterations that prove necessary.

Cut around notches . . .          . . . or cut off and clip.

Don't move the cut pieces or remove the pattern from the fabric until all the necessary marks have been transferred to the fabric.

Save any leftover fabric until you've completed the garment; it comes in handy for test-stitching seams and buttonholes and making covered buttons, belts, or repairs.

# ROTARY CUTTING

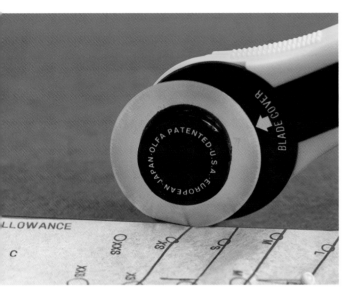

Rotary cutters entered the sewing scene about 30 years ago as quilting tools for quickly cutting strips, triangles, and squares. Rotary cutters, rulers, and self-healing cutting mats have also proven themselves very useful for sewing garments and home decor. Be sure to add these handy tools to your sewing kit.

## ROTARY-CUTTER BASICS

A rotary cutter is similar to a pizza wheel. It has a very sharp circular blade that rotates and is capable of slicing through up to eight fabric layers with an accurate, clean cut. Rotary cutters have a built-in blade-guard system to protect you from the blade when not in use. Some guards are manually clicked into place and others automatically move out of the way when you apply cutting pressure.

Rotary cutters and blades are available in different sizes: 18 mm, 28 mm, 45 mm, 60 mm, and 65 mm. The larger blades are good for cutting through multiple fabric layers and making long, straight cuts. Smaller blades are better for cutting around curves. Small blades become dull more quickly than large blades because of their smaller circumference. To start,

purchase a 28 mm and a 45 mm or 60 mm rotary cutter. If you can only purchase one, buy a 45 mm cutter.

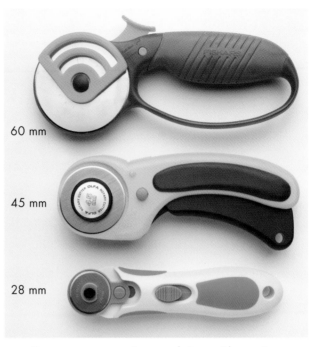

Rotary cutters come in several sizes, with a variety of handle styles and safety mechanisms.

Replacement blades are available. It's a good idea to have extra blades on hand—buy the same brand as your cutter. Follow the manufacturer's instructions to replace the blades for your cutter. If you accidentally roll the blade over a pin, the corner of a ruler, or another hard object, the blade will be damaged and leave portions of the fabric uncut. Blades also become dull with use. If a blade hasn't been changed recently, or you notice more pressure is required to make a cut, it's probably time for a new blade. Dispose of old blades in the packaging from the new blade to protect unsuspecting trash collectors.

Treat your rotary cutter as you'd treat your scissors—use it only for fabric. If you want to cut paper, buy a separate cutter for that purpose.

In addition to the standard flat-blade rotary cutters, you can also purchase decorative blades, such as pinking, squiggle, and scallop. You'll need a special cutter designed to hold these dimensional blades; they won't fit in the standard cutter. They can be useful for seam finishing or for decorative edges, especially on non-raveling fleece and felt. When using them, don't try to keep the blade flush against the ruler. It's very easy to nick the ruler with the protruding blade, causing damage to both.

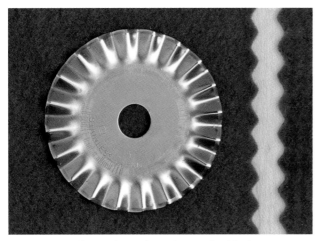

Pinking: Like pinking shears, this blade finishes seams and adds a decorative edge.

Scallop: This blade provides a more dramatic and pronounced wavy edge.

Squiggle: For a very distinct look, try the squiggle blade with its textured points.

## NECESSARY ACCESSORIES

A rotary cutter is used in conjunction with a rotary-cutting mat that's placed on a flat surface. Using a rotary cutter without a mat will damage the blade and destroy your work surface. Many mats are self-healing. This means that after a cut is made, the small slit in the mat comes back together. The surface stays smooth and can be used over and over. The mat also provides a good work surface when using a craft knife.

Mats come in a variety of sizes, from 6" x 8" to 40" x 72". Most have printed grids that are helpful for measuring and squaring fabric. Some mats fold for storage or come in sections that interlock together to form a larger cutting surface. A mat that's at least 24" in one direction is good for cutting yardage—half the fabric width fits in the 24" dimension. If you plan on cutting out garments, you'll want a mat that's at least 24" x 36" so you can cut most garment sections without having to reposition them over the mat. Buy the largest mat you can afford and have space to store; with care, it will last a long time. Store mats flat and away from heat, and clean them periodically to remove fibers and lint that become trapped in the tiny cuts.

Another rotary-cutting tool is a specialty ruler, which is used to square fabric, measure each cut, and guide the cutter. There are many ruler shapes and sizes. Most are made of ⅛"-thick acrylic printed with inch marks and grids. Many rulers also have lines for cutting 30°, 45°, and 60° angles. Always check the marked lines on a new ruler to be sure they're accurate. The imprinted lines aren't always fine lines. To be consistent, align the same side of the ruler line with the fabric edge each time you cut for accurate, same-width strips.

Start your ruler collection with a few basic sizes, such as 6" x 24", 2" x 18" or 3" x 18", and 12"-square rulers. Add to your collection as your experience and needs grow.

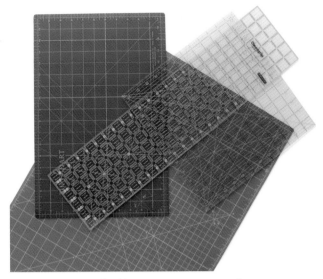

Mats and rulers come in a variety of sizes.

## CUTTING

Instructions are given for right-handed cutting. For left-handed cutting, place the fabric on the opposite side of the ruler and reverse the instructions.

1. Prewash the fabric in the same manner as you plan to care for the finished project. Press the fabric to remove any wrinkles. Use spray starch to add body, if desired.

2. Cut a single fabric layer when you want only one piece. Cut double, triple, or quadruple layers for multiples of one piece.

3. For doubled layers, fold the fabric in half, matching the selvages. The fold should be smooth, even if the cut edges aren't aligned. If the mat is less than 22" wide and you're cutting multiples, fold the fabric in half again by bringing the fold to meet the selvages, making four layers. Place the fabric on the cutting mat with the fold at the top of the mat and the bulk of the fabric to your right.

4. Square the fabric raw edge by aligning one edge of a 12"-square ruler (or an 8½" x11" sheet of paper) with the fold and placing the ruler's left side about 1" from the fabric raw edge. Abut a 6" x 24" ruler next to the square ruler, overlapping the fabric as

shown. Place your left hand firmly on the large ruler to keep it from moving and to compress the fabric layers; remove the square ruler.

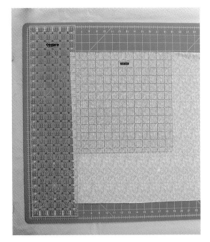

Abut the rulers to ensure a straight cut that's perpendicular to the fold.

### Don't Begin at the End
Extend the ruler beyond the fabric edges to begin cutting at the edge. If you align the ruler with the fabric edge, you may nick the blade on the ruler corner.

5. Hold the cutter in your dominant hand. Keep your arm at a 45° angle from the tabletop and place the rotary blade against the ruler, perpendicular to the cutting surface. Press firmly as you roll the cutter away from you in one continuous motion. The blade must be perpendicular for an accurate cut through all fabric layers.

Press firmly and roll the cutter away from you; never cut toward your body.

6. Measure from the squared fabric end and the folded edge for future cuts. Align the desired measurement mark on the ruler with the fabric edge.

7. Try to position the fabric so you don't have to reposition it after each cut. Sometimes it's easier to place the ruler in a different direction rather than rearranging the fabric. You can make horizontal cuts—just hold the ruler secure and keep the blade perpendicular to the surface. Avoid making cuts toward you; instead, move the fabric for the next cut. If your cutting mat is small enough and is supporting the fabric, move or rotate the whole mat with the fabric to avoid having to square the fabric again.

# MARKING

Transferring the pattern symbols to the fabric aids in construction. Use one of the following methods to mark your fabric.

## SNIPS AND CLIPS

Snipping or clipping into the seam allowance is a quick and easy way to mark notches and darts. Make shallow snips (⅛" to ¼" long) into the seam allowances. Don't cut all the way to the stitching line; this weakens the seam.

When the pattern piece is marked with a single notch, use one snip; for double notches, use two, and so on. Snipping can be used to indicate centerlines, hemlines, and foldlines as well as notches.

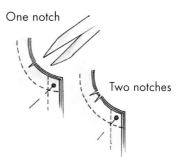

One notch

Two notches

Use ⅛" to ¼" clips to transfer notches to the fabric.

Check the seam-allowance width. If the pattern has ¼" seam allowances, snipping isn't an option; choose another marking method such as cutting outward around the notch.

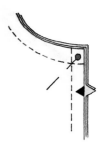

Cut outward notches rather than clipping inward.

## FABRIC-MARKING PENS

Use fabric-marking pens in combination with clipping and notching. For example, clip the dart legs at the seam allowance but draw the dart point with a marking pen. Non-permanent marking pens are also handy for marking embroidery or embellishment placement.

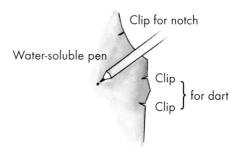

Clip for notch

Water-soluble pen

Clip
Clip } for dart

Use a combination of marking methods.

Air-soluble inks disappear with time; in a humid environment they may disappear too quickly. Water-soluble inks need to be washed away with plenty of clear water—no detergent. Test markers on scrap fabric beforehand; they may behave differently on various fibers, and some are permanently set by heat. When purchasing markers, read the packaging carefully to ensure marks are temporary and to learn removal tips.

## TRACING PAPER

Dressmaker's tracing paper is usually sold in variety packs containing several colors. Choose the paper closest to the fabric color that's still visible on the fabric in case the marks can't be removed completely. A serrated or sawtooth tracing wheel is most commonly used, but a smooth wheel is preferred for delicate fabrics. Work on a self-healing cutting mat or a piece of cardboard to avoid damaging the work surface.

Practice before using a tracing wheel for the first time; learn how much pressure to apply by tracing lines on fabric scraps. Place the paper's colored side against the fabric wrong side, underneath the pattern tissue. Applying slight to moderate pressure, roll the tracing wheel along the lines using a ruler as a guide. Move the tracing paper after each mark to ensure coverage and trace all of the necessary lines. Mark both fabric layers at the same time whenever possible by placing folded tracing paper between the layers; if the fabric has been

folded right sides together for cutting, slip tracing paper both above and below the fabric to mark both layers at once. Mark heavyweight fabrics in single layers to ensure clear marks.

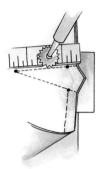

Transfer marks with a tracing wheel and dressmaker's tracing paper using a ruler to guide straight lines.

If you want to trace stitching lines for a multisized pattern where the seamlines aren't marked, first measure and mark the stitching lines on the tissue; then use the tissue as your guide.

Tracing paper isn't the best choice for marking on the fabric right side, and its marks may show through sheer and lightweight fabrics. Weigh the advantages and disadvantages and consider other methods when tracing paper is unsatisfactory.

## TAILOR'S CHALK

This classic marking product works on almost any fabric because it's easily removed and doesn't leave residue. However, easy removability may be a problem for projects that will be handled a lot during construction. Tailor's chalk comes in a variety of colors and has a chalky or waxy consistency. It's available in a flat flake, a powder with an applicator, or in pencil form. The chalky type works best on smooth surfaces while the wax version performs better on textured fabrics such as bouclé or corduroy.

## STRAIGHT PINS

Use straight pins to mark details that will be immediately sewn or basted. They aren't a good long-term marking method since pins may slip out of the fabric with handling.

Use pins to indicate the ends of an opening, placement for a collar, or where to start and stop stitching. Place two pins perpendicular to each other to indicate a corner. Also use pins to mark the ends of buttonholes and the lower stop of a zipper.

Pin-marking isn't recommended for fine fabrics or fabrics that retain pin holes. Use ball-point pins on knit fabrics. Remember not to iron over plastic-headed pins; the plastic may melt and leave permanent spots on the fabric.

## PRESSURE-SENSITIVE STICKERS

Use stickers when ink, chalk, or pins might damage the fabric. Some people find stickers easier than marking, so they use them on all projects. Stickers are typically used to indicate interior pattern marks, such as pocket guidelines, snaps, or buttons. Experiment with stickers found in office-supply stores and draw placement markings on them.

# INTERFACING

Interfacing adds body and creates structure in garments. It stabilizes lightweight fabric and provides support behind buttons and buttonholes. There are three basic types of interfacing: knit, woven, and nonwoven.

**Knit** interfacing preserves a softer, more draped effect.

**Woven** interfacing adds stability and strength.

**Nonwoven** interfacing strengthens base fabric, but may also add stiffness.

Interfacing is available in both fusible and non-fusible (sew-in) types. Fusible interfacing is easy to work with, making it well suited for beginners.

Typically, the interfacing you use should be slightly lighter weight than your fabric. Bolt ends often indicate the appropriate fabric weights or garment types for the interfacing.

## APPLYING INTERFACING

Always follow the manufacturer's instructions when fusing interfacing, as there may be variations among different brands of fusibles. Specific instructions are usually provided on a plastic wrapper that is cut along with the interfacing. However, the following general guidelines usually apply when working with fusible interfacing:

1. Cut each pattern piece to be interfaced from both fabric and interfacing. Follow the pattern instructions for further cuts to the interfacing; often all but ⅛" of the seam allowance is cut away to reduce bulk. Like with fabric, be sure to cut reversed pieces as necessary for right and left sides.

2. Center the interfacing on the fabric, placing the adhesive side (usually rough or shiny) of the interfacing next to the fabric wrong side.

3. Cover the interfacing and fabric with a press cloth. Some interfacings recommend using a damp press cloth.

4. Check the manufacturer's instructions for guidelines on using steam. Place the iron on the interfacing and press down firmly for 10 seconds, without sliding the iron back and forth. Pick the iron up and move it to another position, slightly overlapping the first, and repeat the process until the entire piece is fused.

5. Allow the fabric to cool and dry completely before moving it. Turn the interfaced fabric over and press again from the fabric side to complete the bond.

When working with non-fusible interfacing, follow these general guidelines:

1. Cut the interfacing the same size as the pattern piece to be interfaced.

2. Pin the interfacing to the wrong side of the corresponding fabric piece, matching the raw edges.

3. Baste the interfacing to the fabric by stitching ⅛" inside the seamline (usually ½" from the raw edge).

4. Trim *only the interfacing* close to the basting stitches to remove the excess bulk within the seam allowances.

# SEAMS

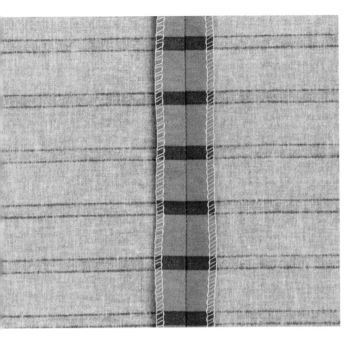

Sewing seams isn't difficult. The pattern instruction sheet and pattern pieces indicate how wide the seam allowances should be; for commercial garment patterns in the U.S., the width is traditionally ⅝", with ⅜" and ¼" sometimes used for small pieces or attaching details. The seam-allowance width may vary within a single pattern piece, so it's always wise to check before you sew.

Here's an overview of the usual method for sewing a plain seam:

1. Place two pieces of fabric right sides together, aligning the cut edges and matching any notches.

2. Pin the edges together, placing the pins perpendicular to the edge and approximately 4" apart.

3. With the pin heads on top, place the fabric under the presser foot. Align the pinned fabric edge with the corresponding seam guideline on the sewing-machine bed.

4. Lower the presser foot. Lower the needle into the fabric by turning the hand wheel or by using the needle-position button if your machine has one.

5. Secure the stitches at the beginning and end of each seam by backstitching. Starting near the raw edge at the end of the seamline, make two or three stitches; then stitch in reverse for two to three stitches. Stitch forward, sewing the remainder of the seam.

6. Stop stitching and remove pins as you near them. Sewing over pins can bend the pins, break the needle, and wear down the machine's feed dogs.

7. Take your time and make sure the fabric edges stay even with the seam guideline on the machine. One way to create an unsatisfactory seam is to sew too quickly. Watch the fabric edge, not the needle.

8. At the end of the seam, backstitch. Sew to within a few threads of the raw edge; then sew in reverse for about ½".

9. Raise the needle by turning the hand wheel or pushing the appropriate button. Raise the presser foot. Pull the fabric toward the back of the machine and trim the threads close to the fabric, leaving 2" to 3" thread tails near the needle.

## PIVOTING

Sewing straight seams is an easily mastered skill. However, there will be times when you need to turn a corner. Pivot at corners using the following technique:

1. Stitch to the corner (the point where two seamlines cross); stop with the needle down in the fabric. Lift the presser foot.

2. Turn the fabric and align the next edge with the stitching guideline on the machine bed.

3. Lower the presser foot and continue stitching.

## SEAM FINISHES

Every seam needs a good finish, and some options are more appropriate for one fabric than another. When you begin a new project, it's a good idea to test different seam finishes on a scrap of the project fabric. The correct seam finish prevents the fabric from raveling and helps the seam stand up to wear and cleaning. A good seam finish should be smooth and without puckers. It shouldn't add much bulk to the seam or show on the project right side.

**Pinked finish.** Use pinking shears to trim along the edge of firmly woven fabrics, cutting away just a few fabric threads (A). For greater stability, stitch ¼" from the edge of each seam allowance separately, and then pink.

**Machine zigzag finish.** This is good for all fabric weights. Set the sewing machine for a wide, open zigzag stitch and sew the seam allowances together near the seamline (B). If desired, trim away the excess fabric close to the zigzag stitches.

**Overcast finish.** This treatment is suitable for all knit and woven fabrics. Sew the two seam allowances together using the overcast stitch on a conventional machine or a serger three-thread overlock so the stitch overlaps the fabric edge (C).

# PRESSING

Although some people use the terms pressing and ironing interchangeably, the two are not the same. Pressing is an up-and-down motion that shapes fabric with pressure and sometimes steam, while ironing is a back-and-forth motion for removing wrinkles. If you use the right tools and learn the proper techniques, pressing can transform a garment's appearance from homemade to professional.

## PRESSING MATTERS TO CONSIDER

- Test scrap fabric first to determine how heat and steam will affect the fabric.

- Press as you sew—don't wait until you finish the project. Never cross a seam, pleat, dart, or tuck with a new row of stitches until it's been pressed.

- Press from the fabric wrong side unless otherwise directed.

- Use a press cloth, if necessary, to protect the fabric, especially when pressing from the right side.

- Press lightly at first to prevent seam allowances from imprinting on the project right side. Use the tip of the iron along the seamline rather than pressing the seam-allowance edges into the fabric.

- Allow the fabric to cool (and dry, if using steam) before moving it.

- Never press over pins or basting. This can leave imprints or dimples that are very difficult to remove. Pressing over pins can also scratch the iron's soleplate or melt plastic pinheads.

## PRESSING AREA

Set up a pressing area near your sewing machine at a comfortable height. For pressing while standing, ergonomic experts suggest setting the ironing surface about 8" below your elbow. For pressing while sitting, place the board at the same height as your sewing table, at a right angle to the sewing machine. An ironing board with adjustable height lets you customize its position whether you're sitting or standing. You'll be more apt to use your pressing tools if they're within easy reach.

# DARTS

Wrong side

Right side

How can you make a flat piece of fabric conform to the contours of a three-dimensional body? The answer is to fold out excess fabric. In garments, this is accomplished with darts. Darts make the difference between an ill-fitting garment and one that accentuates your curves, making you look fabulous.

A dart is a fold of fabric stitched on the wrong side of a garment to create a closer fit. You'll find darts used most often to shape the bust, back, waist, and hips. There are three basic types of darts: single pointed, double pointed, and curved. Each type has a different shape in order to achieve a different result. As a rule, the more curved the dart, the closer it will fit to the body.

Darts appear on commercial patterns as triangles, diamonds, or football shapes, depending on their type. Before cutting out a darted garment, pin-fit the pattern pieces around your body to make sure that each dart points directly toward the fullest part (or parts) of the body to which the pattern is conforming. Redraw the dart to make it longer or shorter, or raise or lower the dart point if necessary to achieve the desired amount of fullness.

Transfer all dart markings to the fabric wrong sides before removing the pattern tissue. See "Marking" on page 10 for details.

## SINGLE-POINTED STRAIGHT DART

This is the most common dart. On a pattern it looks like a triangle with a line through the center.

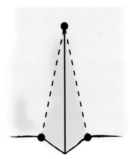

Single-pointed straight dart

1. Mark the dart lines and any matching points (usually indicated on the pattern by small dots) on the fabric wrong side. Be sure to mark the dot at the pointed end of the dart.

2. With the fabric right sides together, fold the dart on the centerline. Make sure the outer lines and matching points align; pin at right angles to the stitching line, placing one pin at the dart point.

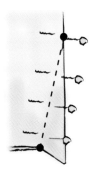

Fold on centerline, matching stitching lines.

3. Stitch from the wide end to the point, making the last two or three stitches as close to the foldline as possible; don't backstitch. Remove the garment piece from the machine, leaving thread tails approximately 4" long.

4. With the thread ends together, tie a knot as close to the dart point as possible.

5. Press the dart fabric toward the center of the garment or as directed in the pattern instructions.

### Keep It Smooth

Leaving long thread tails instead of backstitching prevents a bubble from forming at the dart tip.

## DOUBLE-POINTED STRAIGHT DART

This dart has a point at each end, appearing as an elongated diamond. The double-pointed straight dart can take the place of two single-pointed darts when placed at the waistline. The widest part sits at the waist, with the points toward the bust and hip.

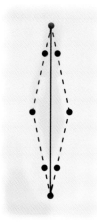

Double-pointed straight dart

1. For accuracy, stitch double-pointed darts in two directions as two separate steps. Mark the dart lines and all matching points on the garment wrong side.

2. With right sides together, fold the dart on the centerline. Match and pin the dart outer lines together, pinning first at the waist point, and then at the end points. Add additional pins as needed.

Fold and pin carefully.

3. Beginning at the center dot, stitch toward one end point, making the last two or three stitches as close to the foldline as possible; don't backstitch. Remove the garment from the machine, leaving thread tails approximately 4" long.

4. Stitch in the opposite direction. Start again from the dart center, overlapping a few stitches of the previous stitching line, and work toward the remaining point. Leave 4" thread tails. Knot the thread tails at each dart end.

5. Clip into the dart fold at the waistline, ending ⅛" from the stitches. Press both halves of the dart toward the garment center. Clipping the dart alleviates strain at the waistline by allowing the dart to lie smooth at the center of the waistline curve.

## CURVED DARTS

Curved darts are stitched very much like straight ones, but because of their shape, curved darts fit closer to the body. On a pattern, a curved dart looks similar to a straight dart, except the stitching lines are curved rather than straight.

Single-pointed curved dart

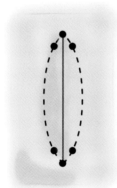

Double-pointed curved dart

1. Mark the dart sewing lines and all matching points on the garment wrong side.

2. With right sides together, fold the dart along its center so the stitching lines and match points align; pin in place.

3. Stitch the dart on the lines and secure the thread tails, following the instructions for either a single- or double-pointed dart.

4. Clip the folded edge perpendicular to the stitching in several places along the curve to prevent puckering, ending the clips ⅛" from the stitching.

## PRESSING DARTS

The steps for pressing darts are simple.

1. Press the dart flat as stitched.

2. Lay the dart over a pressing ham and press the dart to one side. For horizontal darts, such as bust darts, press the fold downward; for vertical darts, press the fold toward the garment center.

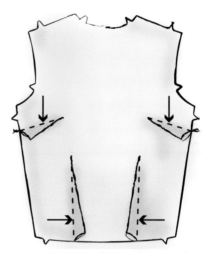

Press horizontal darts down and vertical darts toward garment center.

3. If the dart is wide or the fabric is heavy, slash the dart to within 1" of the point and trim the seam allowances to ½" from the stitching line. Press the slashed allowances open and the point flat.

Slash dart and press the allowance open and the point flat.

# HEMS

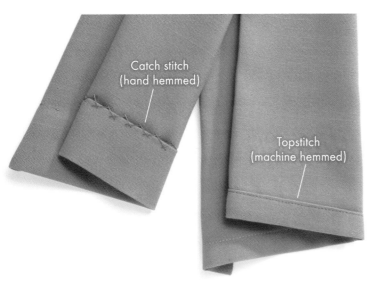

Catch stitch (hand hemmed)

Topstitch (machine hemmed)

There are many ways to stitch hems—some hems are sewn by hand and others by machine; some are invisible, while others showcase decorative stitching. When choosing a method, consider the fabric, the garment style, and your personal preference. Finish the raw edge of the hem allowance before stitching the hem in place.

## HEMMING BY HAND

These stitches are worked either flat or "blind." Flat stitches are visible on the garment wrong side, going over the hem's cut edge and into the garment. Blind stitches are hidden between the hem allowance and the garment.

1. Turn up the hem allowance along the hemline and press the fold. Pin the hem in place through both layers. Pin ¼" below and parallel to the edge, which has already been finished by folding, overcasting, serging, or binding.

2. Thread a hand-sewing needle with no more than 18" of thread that closely matches the fabric. Knot one end and stitch with a single thread. Select one of the following hand stitches to secure the edge. Work on a flat surface, and don't pull the stitches too tight or the hem will ripple.

When stitching into the garment, take the smallest stitch possible, picking up only one or two threads. This will keep the stitches nearly invisible on the garment right side. Secure the first and last stitches with a backstitch or two in the hem allowance, in addition to the initial knot.

Left-handed stitchers may find it easier to work these stitches in the opposite direction. It may be helpful to view the diagrams in a mirror.

**Slant hemming stitch.** This is one of the least-durable hems because so much thread is exposed. Working from right to left, secure the thread on the wrong side of the hem, and then bring it up through the hem edge. Take a stitch into the garment ¼" to ⅜" from the first stitch; then insert the needle into the hem edge the same distance away. The resulting hem resembles a whipstitch.

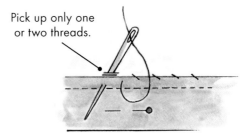

Pick up only one or two threads.

Work slant hemming stitch from right to left.

**Slip stitch.** Select this stitch for hems with folded or bound edges. Working from right to left, bring the first stitch out through the fold of the hem or hem binding and take a small stitch into the garment. Slip the needle into the fold near the tiny stitch and slip it through about ¼" of the hem fold before emerging to make the next stitch.

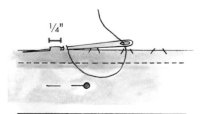

¼"

Work slip stitch from right to left, picking up ¼" of finished hem.

**Catch stitch.** Choose this stitch for hemming knits and stretch fabrics. Working from left to right, fasten the thread on the wrong side of the hem. Take a small right-to-left stitch in the garment fabric, then take the next stitch in the hem approximately ¼" to ⅜" to the right, making sure the thread crosses over itself to create an X.

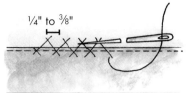

Work catch stitch from left to right.

A blind catch stitch is worked similarly, but between the hem allowance and garment. Roll the hem edge back to work the stitches; pick up only two or three threads in both the garment and hem, and keep the tension even but not too tight.

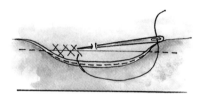

Work blind catch stitch between
the hem allowance and garment.

**Blind hem stitch.** This is the most versatile stitch, and it works well with most hem finishes and fabrics. Working from right to left, fold the hem edge back about ¼" and fasten the thread to it. Take a stitch in the garment fabric, picking up only two or three threads; then take the next stitch into the hem, approximately ¼" away.

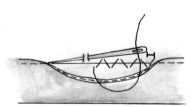

Work blind hem stitch from right
to left between hem and garment.

## MACHINE-STITCHED HEMS

Whether you're looking for an invisible hem or a more decorative one, your sewing machine is faster than stitching by hand.

**Blind hem.** Done correctly, this stitch is sturdy and inconspicuous. It can be used on many fabrics and is especially suitable for gathered skirts and children's clothing. It works best on straight rather than curved

hem edges. The stitch consists of three to six straight (or narrow zigzag) stitches sewn on the hem allowance only, followed by a wide zigzag that barely bites into the garment fabric. Set your machine for a blind hem stitch, and attach the blind hem foot with its special shape to guide the folded hem (consult your machine manual for specifics).

Fold, press, and baste the hem allowance into place. With the wrong side of the garment face up, fold the hem allowance under, leaving the upper ¼" of the hem edge exposed. Place the garment fold to the left of the foot and the hem edge to the right. Stitch along the hem allowance so the wide zigzag barely bites into the fold, catching only two or three threads. If the stitches bite too far into the fold, reduce the stitch width. Choose the alternate stitch, with narrow zigzag stitches in place of the straight ones, for knits and stretch fabrics.

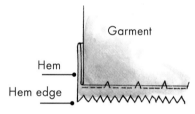

The zigzag barely catches the fold.

**Topstitched hem.** If you're looking for a sporty or casual look, consider a topstitched hem. The hemstitches are visible on the garment right side and can be anything from a single row of straight stitching to several rows of decorative stitching.

For woven fabrics, turn up the hem allowance the desired amount and finish the hem edge by pressing ½" to the wrong side. Hand baste the hem in place along the inner fold. From the garment right side, topstitch just below the basting. Keep the stitching straight and parallel to the hemline. Remove the basting when the topstitching is complete.

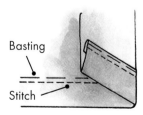

Baste the hem edge from the wrong side;
topstitch from the right side using the basting as a guide.

For knits, especially lightweight ones, use a narrow topstitched hem. Trim the hem allowance to ⅝" and press it to the wrong side along the hemline. Hand baste ½" from the raw edge (near the fold). From the garment right side, stitch ½", and then ⅜" from the hemline fold or use a twin needle to stitch both rows at once. Remove the basting.

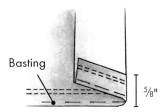

Turn up the hem and baste;
double topstitch in place.

**Narrow hem.** When the hem is narrow and the stitching doesn't need to be hidden, choose this hem treatment. Trim the hem allowance to ½". Press ¼" to the wrong side; then press another ¼" to the wrong side. Stitch along the inner fold.

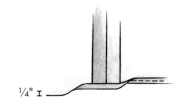

Turn up ¼" twice, and then topstitch.

## Keep It Short
When hand sewing, cut the thread lengths 18" or shorter—any longer and the thread knots and frays easily, causing frustration.

# FACINGS

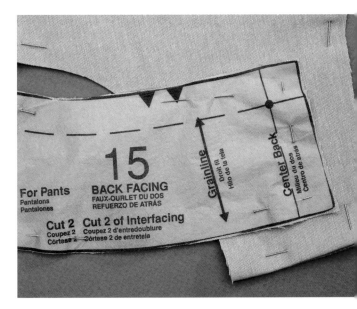

Facings finish the raw edges of armholes and necklines, stabilizing these bias-cut edges and preventing stretching and sagging. Other areas that may require a facing include front and back opening edges. For facings around a zipper, see "Zippered Openings" on page 22.

Facings are sometimes cut as extensions to the garment front or back pattern piece (called "self facings"), but for curved edges, a separate facing piece shaped to match the garment is required. All curved edges have inherent bias stretch, so faced edges require interfacing to add stability and prevent stretching.

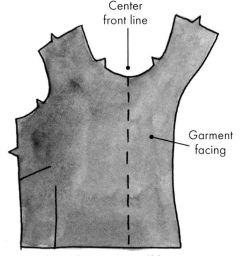

Blouse front with a self facing

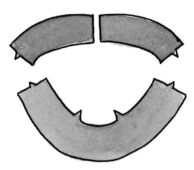

Shaped facing pieces for a
neckline with a center-back seam

Follow these easy steps to ensure smoothly stitched and turned facings on armholes and necklines without zippers.

## INTERFACING

Apply fusible interfacing of the appropriate weight and type to the wrong side of the facing pieces. Some patterns reuse garment pattern pieces for cutting interfacing, while others have separate interfacing patterns.

1. Cut the interfacing and trim all but ⅛" of the interfacing seam allowances. Do not trim the outer edge of the interfacing. Position the interfacing on the facing wrong side, matching the outer edges.

2. Trim any interfacing that extends beyond the facing edges to avoid fusing it to the ironing board. Some directions suggest trimming the interfacing ⅛" to ¼" smaller than the facing pieces along the outer edge; this step isn't necessary, but is a precaution to prevent fusing the facing to the ironing board. Fuse the interfacing, following the manufacturer's instructions.

## CONSTRUCTION

1. Stay stitch ½" from the curved raw edges of the garment to prevent stretching.

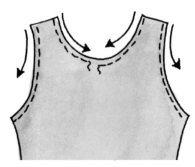

Stay stitch curved edges to be faced.

2. Sew the front and back facing pieces, right sides together, at the shoulder seams for a neckline facing or at the shoulder and underarm for an armhole facing. Trim the seam allowances to ¼" to reduce bulk in the finished garment.

3. Finish the facing's unnotched outer edge using one of the methods in "Edge-Finishing Options" on page 23.

4. With right sides together, pin the facing to the garment, matching notches, centers, and seamlines. Stitch along the seamline; then press the stitching line to set the stitches.

5. Trim the seam allowances to ¼", and then trim only the facing seam allowance to ⅛". This step is called "grading" and prevents ridges along the finished edge.

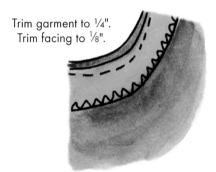

Trim garment to ¼".
Trim facing to ⅛".

Grade the seam allowances.

6. For a smooth turn, clip the inward curves. Clip sparingly, and stagger clips between the layers to prevent show-through or weakening of the seam.

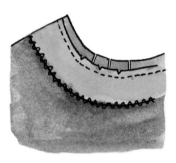

Clip sparingly, staggering the clips.

Over-clipping weakens the seamed edge. This step may not be necessary on wide shallow curves, but is essential for tighter curves, such as underarm curves or the shoulder area in a jewel neckline. When facing outward curved edges, cut notches rather than clips to remove fullness in the seam allowance. An easy way to do this is to use pinking shears when trimming the seam allowances.

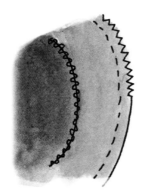

Notch outward curves by cutting with pinking shears.

7. Press the facing and seam allowances away from the garment, and then edgestitch the facing to the seam allowances. Don't overlook this step, called understitching; it controls the facing edge so it won't roll or flip to the garment right side.

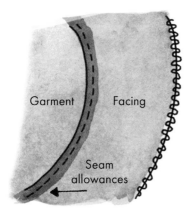

Garment  Facing

Seam allowances

Understitch the facing to the seam allowances.

8. Turn the facing to the garment wrong side and press carefully, rolling the seam just slightly to the wrong side. If you're pressing a rounded neckline or armhole facing, use a pressing ham.

9. Tack the facings to the garment seam allowances using one of the following methods:
   - Whipstitch the facing to the seam allowances only.
   - Pin the facing in place. Working from the right side, stitch in the ditch of the shoulder and/or underarm seams for the width of the facing.
   - Fuse lightweight fusible-web tape between the garment and facing at the seamlines to anchor the facings.

## ZIPPERED OPENINGS

1. Apply fusible interfacing to the facing wrong side. See "Interfacing" on page 12.

2. Finish the facing's unnotched outer edge using one of the methods in "Edge-Finishing Options" on page 23.

3. Insert the zipper according to the pattern guide sheet. Unzip the zipper.

4. With right sides together, pin the facing to the garment edge and snugly wrap the facing ends around the zipper tape. Stitch the facing to the neckline, catching the folded facing ends. Grade the seam allowances and trim the corners to reduce bulk.

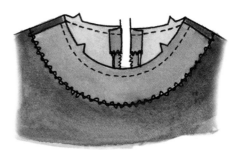

Wrap the facing ends around the zipper tape and stitch.

5. Understitch the facing, beginning and ending the stitching as far as possible into the turned corners at the zipper edges. Turn the facing to the garment wrong side.

6. At the zipper opening, turn under the facing raw edges, pin to the zipper tape, and slip-stitch in place. Add a hook and eye above the zipper.

Slip-stitch the facing ends to the zipper tape; add a hook-and-eye closure.

## EDGE-FINISHING OPTIONS

Serging or zigzagging is the easiest and least-bulky method for finishing the raw edge of a woven fabric facing. With a serger, use a three-thread overlock stitch of medium width and length. Serge the raw unnotched edges after applying the fusible interfacing and before attaching the facing to the garment. If zigzagging with a conventional machine, choose a medium-width open zigzag. Use an accessory foot with a metal pin designed to prevent tunneling if one is available for your machine.

It's easier to finish a facing edge when the facing is flat. For an armhole facing or a neckline facing, stitch the front and back facing together at one seam. Trim the seam allowances to ¼"; press. Serge the unnotched outer edge. Stitch the remaining seam, trim, and press.

Pattern guide sheets often direct you to clean-finish the facing edge. To clean-finish, press ¼" to the wrong side along the unnotched outer edge and edgestitch to secure. To make this easier, machine baste ¼" from the raw edge, and then turn the raw edge under along the basting. This finish isn't recommended for heavier fabrics because it adds a bulky ridge visible on the garment right side at the facing edge.

A Hong Kong finish gives a very tailored look. Cut 1"-wide bias strips of a lightweight fabric, such as China silk or organza. With the raw edges even and right sides together, stitch the strip to the right side of the unnotched facing edge using a ¼" seam allowance. Press the bias strip toward the seam allowance, and then wrap it over the raw edge to the wrong side. From the facing right side, stitch in the ditch to secure the bias strip's raw edge. Because the binding is cut on the bias, the raw edge won't ravel.

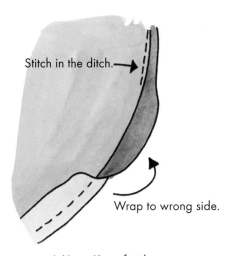

Stitch in the ditch.→

Wrap to wrong side.

A Hong Kong finish

Knit fabric facings don't require an edge finish, but you may want to stitch and pink the edge for a more finished look. Stitch ¼" from the raw edge, and then use pinking shears to trim the edge. This finish can also be used on firmly woven fabrics, if binding or serging aren't desired; fusible interfacing will retard fraying on all but the most loosely woven materials.

### Shapely Facings
Place the facing on the ironing board and lay the pattern over it to make sure the fabric hasn't been distorted from moving it. Adjust if necessary. Remove the pattern piece, position the interfacing on the fabric, and fuse in place according to the manufacturer's instructions.

## GETTING AROUND CORNERS

A smooth finish on a square neckline is a little trickier than on curved necklines.

1. Reinforce the neckline corners before applying the facing. Adjust the machine for a short straight stitch (1.5 to 2 mm long).

2. At each corner of the neckline, stay stitch just inside the seam allowance for 1" on either side of the corner pivot points.

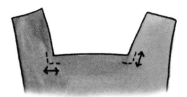

Stay stitch for 1" on each side of corners.

3. Stitch the facing to the garment and grade the seam allowances. At the corners, clip all the way to, but not through, the stitching.

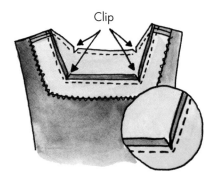

Clip

Stitch the facing to the garment; clip into the corners.

4. Press the seam allowances and facing away from the garment. Understitch the facing as far as possible into the corners; then turn the facing to the wrong side and press. Tack the facing to the garment seam allowances.

# GATHERING

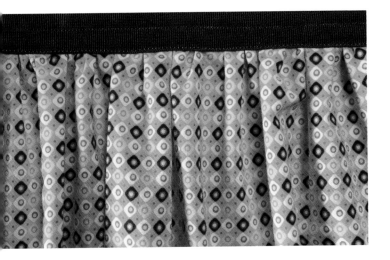

In just a few easy steps, you can transform a flat piece of fabric into one with shape, movement, and grace. Gathering is often seen at garment waistlines, cuffs, yokes, and sleeves, or as ruffles. It's also used in home-decor projects, such as bedskirts and window treatments. Gathering allows you to fit a long piece of fabric (such as a full skirt) onto a shorter piece of fabric (such as a waistband). The result is soft, evenly spaced folds that add shape to the project.

The best method to use for gathering depends on the amount of fabric to be gathered.

## GATHERING A SMALL AREA

1. Set the sewing machine for a straight stitch 4.0 mm long and loosen the needle thread tension slightly. Working from the right side, machine stitch two rows of basting, ¾" and ½" from the edge. Leave long thread tails at each end; do not use the machine's automatic thread cutter.

2. Gather the edge to the desired length by pulling the bobbin threads with one hand while evenly distributing the fullness with the other hand. It's helpful to work from both ends toward the center.

3. Secure the basting threads at each end by wrapping the bobbin thread ends in a figure eight around a pin placed perpendicular to the seamline.

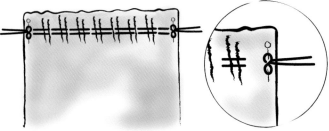

Wrap the gathering threads around a pin in a figure-8 fashion.

4. To secure the gathers, stitch ⅝" from the edge, between the rows of gathering stitches, keeping the gathers smooth and evenly distributed. Stitch again ⅜" from the edge. Remove the basting thread that's visible from the right side.

## GATHERING LARGE AREAS

When gathering yards of fabric (such as gathering an edge for a dust ruffle), use this method, which eliminates the possibility of the basting thread breaking.

1. Working on the fabric wrong side, place a length of lightweight string or narrow cord just inside the seamline of the edge to be gathered. Fishing line can also be used.

2. Stitching within the seam allowance and being careful not to catch the string in the stitching, zigzag over the string.

Zigzag over string just inside the seamline.

3. Pull the string, sliding the zigzag stitches and fabric along its length, to gather the edge. Secure the string using the figure-eight method.

4. Stitch the gathers in place on both sides of the zigzag stitching. Remove the string to eliminate bulk; the zigzag stitching won't show and doesn't need to be removed.

**Weighing In on Gathers**
Use the first gathering method for lightweight fabrics and the second for heavy or stiff fabrics.

# SHIRRING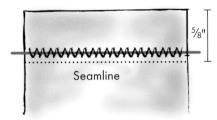

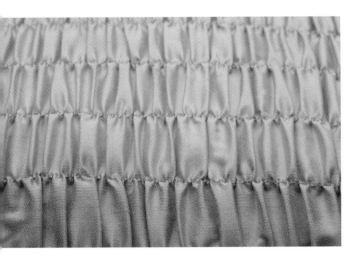

Shirring is a method of creating decorative fabric gathers along two or more parallel stitching lines. Add dimensional interest to any home-decor project or garment by shirring fabric before construction.

1. Determine the finished dimensions for the shirred-fabric project. Cut the fabric at least twice those dimensions, and add two inches along each edge for a generous seam allowance. For example, to make a 16"-square shirred pillow, double the dimensions (16 x 2 = 32). Then add 2" to each edge (32 + 2 + 2 = 36). So you'd cut a 36" fabric square. Since fabric types gather differently, it's best to experiment on a fabric scrap first to see how much it shrinks when shirred.

2. Lay the cut fabric on a flat surface and smooth out any wrinkles. Use a ruler and air- or water-soluble marking pen to draw stitching lines 1" apart across the fabric, marking only between the 2" seam allowances. Once you've learned the basic technique, experiment with different designs by spacing lines closer together or farther apart.

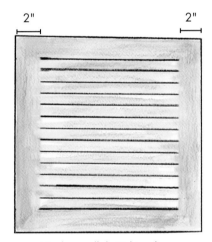

Mark parallel stitching lines.

3. Wind elastic thread onto the bobbin by hand, stretching the elastic slightly as you wind.

4. Insert the bobbin into the machine as normal, and thread the machine with matching all-purpose thread. Do not thread the machine with elastic thread; use it in the bobbin only. Pull the bobbin thread through the throat plate and grasp both the needle thread and the elastic, leaving at least 3" thread tails behind the presser foot. Set the machine for a 3.5 mm or 4.0 mm stitch length.

5. Place the fabric on the sewing machine and position the needle at one end of the first marked stitching line. Lower the needle into the fabric and hold the thread tails prior to stitching.

6. Stitch along one row; do not backstitch at the beginning or end of the row. Clip both the bobbin and top thread 3" from the fabric, also leaving 3" thread tails to begin the next row of stitches.

### Match Point
Use black elastic to shirr dark fabrics and white for lighter fabrics.

7. On the fabric wrong side, tug on the elastic thread tail until you see a loop of upper thread coming through. Pull the loop to bring the upper thread tail to the fabric wrong side. Knot the thread with the elastic, then clip the thread tails close to the knot. Be sure to tie off the thread tails securely at the beginning and end of each stitched row.

8. Continue stitching until all the rows are complete. If the bobbin elastic runs out, snip the top thread and pull it through to the wrong side; tie off. Wind more elastic onto the bobbin, and then begin stitching where you left off. As you stitch more rows, the fabric may bunch, making it difficult to see the stitching line. If this happens, stop stitching and, with the needle down, lift the presser foot and smooth out the fabric. Lower the presser foot and continue stitching.

9. When the stitching is complete and the thread tails are secured on the wrong side, hold a steam iron directly above the shirring on the fabric right side and steam for approximately 10 seconds without bringing the iron into contact with the fabric. Steam causes the elastic to shrink and the shirring to pucker, adding fullness.

# TUCKS

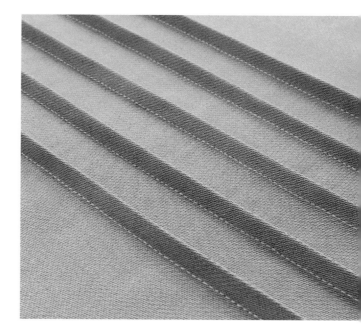

Create texture on clothing and accessories by adding tucks. This simple technique is commonly found on the front of tuxedo shirts and is popping up all over ready-to-wear clothing. Tucks are easy to sew and lend a touch of class to your project.

## SEWING AND PRESSING

1. Cut a 10" fabric square to stitch a few sample tucks.

2. Choose a disappearing pencil or marker that will not be heat set by pressing, and test on scrap fabric first. Then mark a vertical line, following the fabric threads. Tucks often follow the vertical direction of the fabric threads or straight of grain, depending on the design. Mark two more lines, 1½" apart and parallel to the first line.

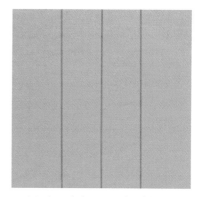

Mark tuck lines on the fabric.

3. With wrong sides together, fold the fabric along the first line. Stitch ¼" (or the distance from the needle to the presser foot edge—what's really important is consistent width) from the fold along the full length of the fabric square. Press the tuck flat, as stitched. Unfold the fabric; press the tuck to one side and flat against the background fabric.

| Stitch the tuck and press as stitched. | Press the tuck to one side. |

4. Repeat the same process with the next two lines, folding, stitching, and pressing each tuck in the same direction as the first. You can see the texture taking shape. Also notice that the width of the square is no longer 10" because each tuck takes up fabric in the same way as a pleat.

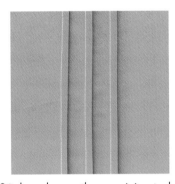

Stitch and press the remaining tucks.

5. For each tuck you plan to make, add two times the width of the tuck to the fabric amount needed. For example, if you're making ¼"-wide tucks, allow ½" of extra fabric for each tuck.

6. Remove the drawn tuck lines according to the marker or pencil manufacturer's directions.

## TUX TUCKS

Tuxedo shirts feature rows of three or more tucks on each side of the button band in the front. The tucks usually range from ¼"- to ¾"-wide when finished.

Some tuxedo shirts have a rectangular or curved panel with tucks on each side of the button band. In this case, it's easy to stitch and press the tucks on separate pieces of fabric, and then cut the panel shapes from the tucked fabric.

Treat the tucked panels normally when stitching them into the other front pieces, taking care to keep each tuck pressed in the correct direction at the seamlines. If the tucks lift off the surface and are hard to keep smooth, stay stitch the tucks flat to the background fabric piece ⅛" from the seamline, within the seam allowance.

## PIN TUCKS

For a variation on tucks, experiment with pin tucks. As their name implies, they're only as wide as a pin.

Pin tucks were very popular in the early twentieth century. They can be vertical or horizontal, or a combination of both can be used to make a crosshatched design. Pin tucks are so fine they can create waves and curves. During the 1930s, very skillful dressmakers created pictures by pin tucking cityscapes, portrait silhouettes, and other designs in handkerchiefs, skirt hems, and table runners.

The process for making pin tucks is the same as for tuxedo tucks. Fold the fabric along the marked line with wrong sides together. Sew approximately 1/16" from the fold with a medium stitch length; stitches that are too short make the pin tuck stiff. Press the tuck flat, as sewn, and then press it to one side with the fabric unfolded.

## BEYOND DECORATION

In addition to adding texture and decoration, tucks can be used to take in fullness and define the fit of a garment. Apply a series of tucks at the end of a sleeve to cinch fabric around the wrist. Instead of darts in a blouse, sew triplets of tucks to take in fabric at the waist. For great ideas, notice how tucks are used in vintage clothing.

Once you've conquered the basics of tucks, play with the effects you can achieve by stitching tucks on striped fabric. Depending on the width of the stripe and the tuck, certain colors can be blocked out or condensed in a specific area for an interesting visual effect.

# COLLARS

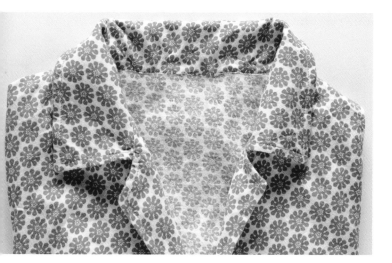

Collars come in all shapes and sizes, but the basic construction process is similar for most of them. Even if you've never attempted a collared garment, a couple of test runs will have you making professional-looking collars in no time. The following construction methods detail the preparation and application of a standard shirt collar with a separate stand (also called the "band"). See additional details on flat collars (Peter Pan) and standing collars (Mandarin) on pages 32 and 31, respectively.

A standard shirt collar has four pieces: two collar pieces (an upper collar and undercollar) and two stand pieces (the stand and the stand facing). The collar pattern, however, has only two pieces; the undercollar is cut using the collar pattern and the stand facing from the stand pattern. Some styles combine the stand and collar in a single pattern piece. Alternate collar styles consist of only the stand (Mandarin) or the collar (Peter Pan).

## INTERFACING SELECTION

Generally, patterns suggest interfacing the undercollar. However, for garments made in lightweight or sheer fabrics, you may want to interface the upper collar instead to prevent seam show-through on the finished collar.

Cut the collar interfacing as directed in the pattern guide sheet. Trim the interfacing diagonally across the collar points just inside the seamline. This eliminates an extra layer of bulk at the already crowded collar point. Fuse the interfacing to the appropriate collar pieces.

Apply interfacing to one collar stand or to both if you prefer a stiffer neckband.

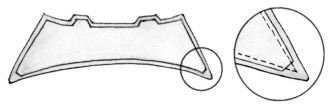

Fuse interfacing to one collar piece.

## ASSEMBLING THE COLLAR

1. On the undercollar, trim ¹⁄₁₆" to a scant ⅛" from the unnotched outer edges. This allows for the "turn of cloth" and helps prevent the undercollar edges from rolling to the outside. This is an essential step for other collar styles as well.

Trim ¹⁄₁₆" to ⅛" from the undercollar edges.

2. With right sides together and the unnotched edges aligned, pin together the upper and undercollar, easing in the extra upper-collar fabric as necessary. Begin stitching at the notched edge of one short end, stopping 1" from the collar point with the needle in the fabric. Shorten the stitch length to 1.4 to 1.6 mm (15 to 18 stitches per inch). Stitch to the corner point, pivot, and take two short stitches across the point. Pivot again, stitch for 1" along the adjacent collar edge, and then return to the normal stitch length. Continue stitching to within 1" of the remaining collar point and repeat the process.

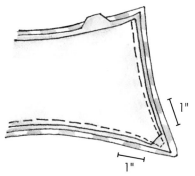

Shorten stitch length and take
two stitches across the collar point.

3. Press the seam to set the stitches. Trim the under-collar seam allowance to ⅛" and the upper-collar allowance to ¼" to grade the seam allowances. Taper the seam allowances to the corners and clip across the corners just outside the stitching. Press the collar seam allowances open as far into the points as possible. If you have a point presser, use it to reach into the corners.

Press the seam allowances open using a point presser if available.

4. Turn the collar right side out and press so the upper collar rolls slightly to the underside. Use a point turner to turn the collar smoothly without poking holes at the corners; press. If desired, edgestitch or topstitch the finished edges to hold the layers together.

## PREPARING THE STAND

1. On the non-interfaced collar stand (stand facing), press the seam allowances on the long edge with single notches to the wrong side; for more control, baste close to the fold. Trim the turned allowance to ⅜". Set the facing aside.

Press seam allowances to the wrong side, baste, and trim to ⅜".

2. Pin the collar raw edge to the interfaced stand's upper edge with the undercollar against the right side of the stand. Match the collar edges to the center-front markings on the stand; baste.

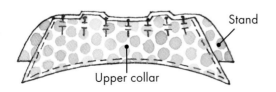

Pin the collar to the stand.

3. Pin the stand facing to the stand, sandwiching the collar between the layers and matching the raw edges; stitch. Trim and grade the seam, leaving the seam allowance of the stand facing (the piece without interfacing) the widest. Notch out the fullness in the curved areas of the stand seam.

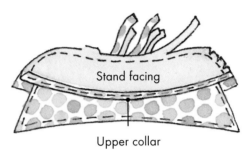

Stitch, grade the seam allowances, and notch the curves.

4. Turn the stand and facing right side out and press them away from the collar.

## ATTACHING TO THE GARMENT

1. Stay stitch the garment front and back necklines ½" from the edge. Complete the garment center-front opening following the pattern instructions.

2. Sew the garment fronts to the back at the shoulder. Clip the curved neckline to the stay stitching; this allows you to straighten the edge so it will fit the collar band smoothly.

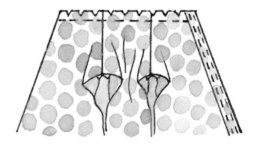

Clip the neckline edge to the stay stitching.

3. Pin the stand to the neckline with right sides together and the notches and dots matching. Fold the stand facing's center-front seam allowances out of the way and stitch the stand to the garment.

Keeping the seam allowances free of the stitching eliminates a bulky edge at the center front.

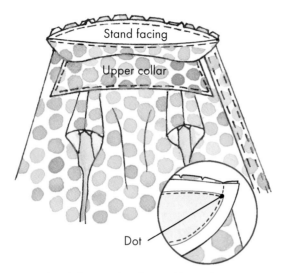

Stitch the stand to the neckline edge.

4. Trim and grade the seam allowances, leaving the stand seam allowances the widest. Press the seam allowances toward the collar.

5. On the garment wrong side, pin the folded edge of the stand facing in place along the stitching line and slip-stitch in place.

Slip-stitch the stand facing
to the garment wrong side.

6. Press the completed collar from the outside. Edgestitch or topstitch the stand edges, beginning and ending the stitching along the stand upper edge; when the collar is folded down, it will hide the point where the stitching begins and ends. Make a horizontal buttonhole in the band and vertical buttonholes down the center-front placket when the shirt is complete.

Begin and end the topstitching
along the stand upper edge.

## ONE-PIECE COLLAR AND STAND

Some shirt patterns have a collar and stand combined into one pattern piece. This kind of collar is simpler to construct and sew to the neckline.

To apply the one-piece shirt collar, follow the interfacing and collar-assembly guidelines for a two-piece collar. Interface the undercollar/stand piece. Prepare the lower edge of the upper-collar/stand facing as described in step 1 of "Assembling the Collar" on page 28. Stitch the collar/stand piece to the neckline and finish by slip-stitching the facing along the stitching.

One-piece stand and collar pattern

## Mandarin Collar

The Mandarin collar, or standing collar, is similar in shape to the stand portion of a shirt collar, and is composed of two pieces—a collar and a matching facing. It may button, or the finished edges may meet at the center front, requiring a neckline-facing finish.

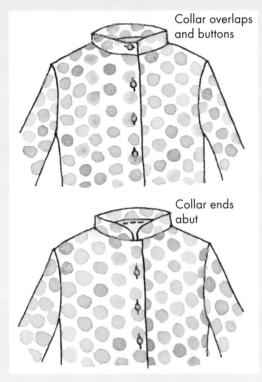

Collar overlaps and buttons

Collar ends abut

Two versions of a standing collar

- If the collar buttons, it's prepared, assembled, and attached to the garment neckline like a collar band, except there isn't a collar sandwiched in the stand seam. Understitch the seam allowance of the upper edge as far into the front ends as possible to help control the upper edge; edgestitching through all layers is another option.

- If the collar edges abut at the center front, interface one collar layer and stitch the layers together along the unnotched edges. Trim and grade the seam allowances, notching curves or trimming corners. Turn the collar right side out and press. Baste the collar to the neckline edge with right sides together, apply the facing, and understitch.

- Some standing collars are made with one piece folded to form both the outside collar and the facing, but the construction method remains essentially the same.

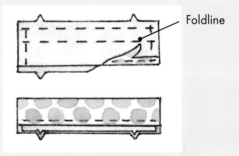

Foldline

A standing collar can also be made in one piece.

## Peter Pan Collar

The Peter Pan collar is a flat collar style most often found on children's clothing. Its name comes from the 1904 play written by James M. Barrie, in which the rounded collars appeared on costumes. It's constructed from either one or two sections with rounded center-front (CF) edges. The flat collar is one of the easiest collars to construct because it's simply caught in the neckline seam with a facing.

Trim the seam allowances with pinking shears to eliminate excess fabric at the curves.

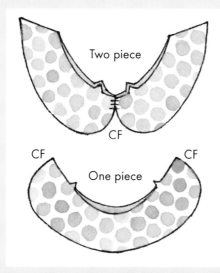

Two- and one-piece Peter Pan collars

When constructing a Peter Pan collar, it's essential to notch out the excess fullness in the outer curved edges; this can be done efficiently with a pair of pinking shears. For a sharply pressed outer edge, understitch the undercollar to the seam allowances after you turn the collar right side out. For more information on understitching, see step 7 on page 22.

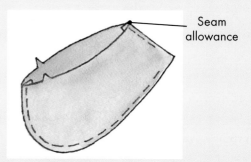

Seam allowance

Understitch the collar.

1. Pin the collar to the stay-stitched garment neckline, right sides up, matching notches and other construction markings; baste.

2. With right sides together, pin the facing on top, matching all marks and sandwiching the collar between; sew through all layers.

3. Trim and grade the seam allowances and press them toward the facing.

4. Understitch the facing to the seam allowances; then press the collar and facing toward the garment.

# SET-IN SLEEVES

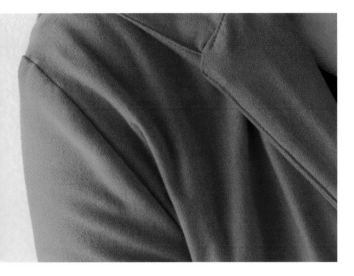

The extra fullness built into a fitted sleeve cap is about 1" to 1½". Some firm fabrics, such as faux suede, don't ease well, and there may be too much fullness for the sleeve to fit smoothly into the armhole without puckers. To remove some of the fullness, flatten the cap a bit on each side of the shoulder dot. Use a French-curve ruler to adjust the cutting line. This alteration won't affect the sleeve length.

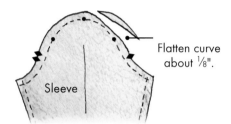

Flatten curve about ⅛".

Sleeve

Lower the sleeve cap slightly to remove extra fullness.

Marking with small snips is more accurate than trying to cut around the notches. When cutting out the garment and sleeve pattern pieces, cut straight across the notches and make ⅛"-long snips into the fabric edge at all dots and notches to mark the fabric. For the back notches make two snips, one through the center of each notch. (Notches are shown in how-to illustrations for clarity only.)

## SETTING THE SLEEVE

1. Follow the pattern guide sheet to assemble the garment body and sew and finish the shoulder and side seams.

2. Prepare to set the sleeve into the armhole. Working on the right side of each sleeve cap, machine baste along the ⅝" seamline and again ¼" away in the seam allowance, beginning and ending both rows of stitching just below the front and back notches. You may choose to lengthen the stitch and/or loosen the needle thread tension. Don't backstitch; leave long thread tails. The bobbin thread will be

Learning to set a smooth, fitted sleeve into an armhole without puckers or twisting is an essential sewing skill for creating professional-looking garments.

Set-in sleeves have a rounded sleeve cap that measures somewhat larger than the armscye, or armhole, it fits into. The extra amount is eased into the seam so the sleeve fits smoothly and the fabric cups slightly over the seam allowances and the shoulder.

The sleeve cap and the front and back pattern pieces have a number of markings to assist in easing the sleeve correctly. The large dot at the top of the sleeve cap aligns with the garment shoulder seam. There's a smaller dot on either side of the shoulder dot, which matches a corresponding dot marked on the armscye of the front and back bodice patterns. Below the dot there's a single notch for the sleeve front and a double notch for the back.

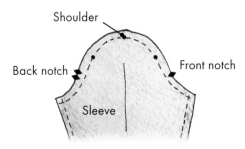

Shoulder

Back notch          Front notch

Sleeve

Dots and notches have corresponding marks on the garment armhole.

on the fabric wrong side. Make sure to reverse one sleeve so you have right and left sleeves.

Machine baste between
notches on the sleeve right side.

3. Stitch the sleeve underarm seam, finish as desired, and press.

4. With the garment wrong side out and the sleeve right side out, slip a sleeve into the corresponding armhole with right sides together. Match the dots, notches, and the underarm seams; pin. You should have six pins placed—one at each of the key matching points. Pin the underarm area between the notches.

5. Pull only the bobbin threads to draw up just enough fullness to fit the sleeve into the armscye. Work from both ends of the basting stitches, easing toward the shoulder, to avoid distorting the grainline. Wrap the thread ends around a pin in a figure eight to secure. Adjust the fullness evenly and pin to hold the slight gathers in place for stitching; the fabric should be flat along the seamline, between the rows of basting.

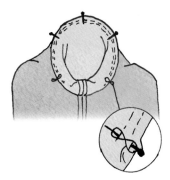

Pin the sleeve into the armhole
and draw up basting stitches.

6. Stitch the sleeve in place, removing pins as you approach them. For best results, stitch with the sleeve side up so you can see and control the fullness to prevent small tucks. Use your fingers to control the eased fullness as you stitch.

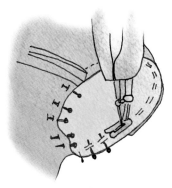

Stitch the armhole seam
with the sleeve side up.

7. On the garment right side, check to make sure there are no tucks in the sleeve seam. If there's a tuck, remove the stitching at the tuck and a little extra on each side of it, adjust the fullness, repin, and stitch again.

8. Stitch the underarm again between the front and back notches, ¼" from the seamline within the seam allowance. Trim the seam allowances close to the stitching in the underarm only. This removes some of the bulk so the sleeve doesn't bind in the underarm.

Stitch again between notches, ¼" inside the
seam allowance. Trim close to the stitches.

9. With the iron tip, gently press the stitches in the sleeve cap to set them and steam out any excess fullness. Turn the seam allowances toward the sleeve, but don't press the area flat. The sleeve cap should cup smoothly over the seam allowances at the shoulder.

## FLAT SLEEVE CAPS

Sleeves with flat caps have little or no ease added. They can be sewn into an open armhole prior to sewing the side seam. Camp shirts, menswear-style shirts for both men and women, and garments with dropped shoulders typically feature this type of sleeve.

1. Sew the garment shoulder seam and finish as desired or as directed in the pattern guide sheet; press.

Sew fronts to back at shoulders.

2. With right sides together, pin the sleeve to the armhole, matching the shoulder, dots, and notches. If there is too much ease to easily pin in, machine baste between the front and back notches as for a set-in sleeve.

3. Stitch the sleeve in place from the garment side with the sleeve against the machine. The feed dogs will ease in the extra fullness as you stitch, resulting in a smooth curve.

4. Stitch again ¼" from the first stitching line, inside the seam allowance, along the entire seam; trim the seam allowances close to the second stitching line below the notches. Press the seam

allowances toward the sleeve or as directed by the guide sheet.

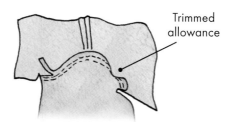

Stitch sleeve ¼" from original seamline; trim.

5. With right sides together, pin and stitch the underarm and side seams in one continuous operation.

Sew underarm and side seams in one operation.

# ZIPPERS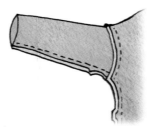

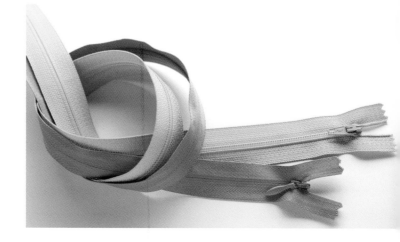

One of the most satisfying sewing skills to master is the ability to insert a zipper quickly and easily with professional-looking results. Whether you choose a centered, lapped, or invisible application, practicing the following methods will calm your fears about making a project that requires a zipper.

# CENTERED ZIPPER

The most common zipper opening is centered down the front or back of a garment. Also, zippers placed in purses, pillows, and other items usually use a centered application. Centered zippers are ideal for everyday clothes, especially for fabric that's heavyweight, has thick pile, or needs to be matched at the seam.

In a centered closure, the zipper is concealed by two flaps of fabric, one on each side of the zipper. When completed, two lines of stitching (one on each side of the zipper) are visible from the right side.

1. Placement for the lower zipper stop is usually marked on the pattern. Stitch the garment seam with a normal stitch length below this mark, backstitching at the mark. Above the mark, machine baste the seam. Press the entire seam open.

2. With the garment wrong side up, place the closed zipper right side down on the seam allowances with the zipper teeth centered along the basted seamline and the upper zipper stop 1" below the garment's upper raw edge. Pin the zipper in place through the seam allowances only; don't pin through to the outside of the garment.

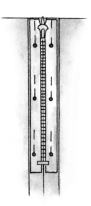

Pin zipper in place through
seam allowances only.

3. Using a zipper foot, baste the zipper to the seam allowances only.

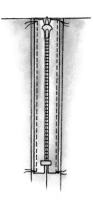

Baste zipper tape to
seam allowances only.

4. For best topstitching results, use a stitch slightly longer than regular sewing, but not as long as a basting stitch. Be careful to stitch an even distance from the teeth. If this is difficult, use a topstitching guide, or center ½"-wide transparent tape along the seam and stitch just beyond the tape edges. Working from the garment right side, topstitch the zipper in place using a zipper foot. To prevent ripples, sew both sides of the zipper in the same direction. Begin at the zipper upper edge and stitch to the end of the basted seamline; then pivot and stitch over to the seamline. Don't backstitch; instead, leave a thread tail to pull to the wrong side. Repeat to sew the zipper's opposite side.

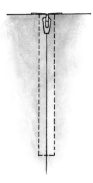

Topstitch the zipper
on both sides.

5. Use a hand-sewing needle to pull the thread ends to the wrong side and tie off. Remove the basting stitches and press with a cool iron.

# LAPPED ZIPPER

When zippers first became popular, most were sewn with a lapped closure. Lapping a zipper hides the teeth better, which is why it's often the application of choice for dressy clothing or when the zipper color doesn't match the fabric exactly. It's also an excellent choice for delicate fabric or pile fabrics that can catch in the zipper teeth.

A lapped zipper is concealed by a fabric flap; only one stitching line is visible from the right side. Lapped zippers are often used in the left side seams of women's pants and skirts.

1. For a lapped zipper, the seam allowances should be at least ⅝" wide. Stitch the garment seam below the lower stop mark with a normal stitch length and machine baste the seam above the mark. Press the seam allowances open.

2. With the garment wrong side up, place the closed zipper right side down on the seam allowances, with the top stop 1" below the garment's upper raw edge. Align the left edge of the zipper tape with the raw edge of the left seam allowance and pin in place through the seam allowance only. Using a zipper foot and a ¼" seam allowance, stitch the zipper tape to the seam allowance only.

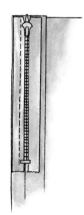

Stitch the zipper tape to
the seam allowance only.

3. Flip the zipper to the left so it's face up. This will create a fold in the seam allowance, but not in the zipper tape. Bring this fold close to (but not touching) the zipper coils. Sew the zipper in place by edgestitching along the fold.

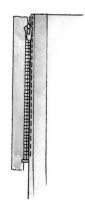

Edgestitch the fabric fold
beside the zipper teeth.

4. Smooth the garment over the zipper, right side up. From the garment right side, topstitch the left-hand side of the zipper (the overlap), starting at the lower end and leaving long thread tails. Slowly stitch across the zipper; then pivot and stitch up the left side, ⅜" from the seamline.

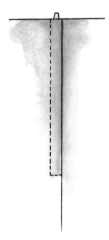

Topstitch the left-hand
side of the zipper.

5. Pull the thread ends to the wrong side and tie off. Remove the basting stitches and press with a cool iron.

# INVISIBLE OR HIDDEN ZIPPER

Invisible zippers make the zipper application look like a seam, and are often substituted for conventional zippers. Unlike a centered or lapped zipper, an invisible zipper is inserted into a fully open seam.

1. When inserting an invisible zipper, it's helpful to use a foot with a groove on the underside that makes the zipper coil stand away from the tape while stitching (invisible zipper foot or pintuck foot). However, you can also use a regular presser foot or zipper foot. A zipper foot is required for the final step. Using a regular presser foot over the zipper coil may keep the foot from lowering completely, preventing the tension discs from being engaged on some machines, causing looped or skipped stitches. In that case, use a zipper foot (either conventional or invisible).

2. Mark the stitching lines on each garment piece by pressing under the seam allowances or basting along the seamline where the zipper will be inserted. Open the zipper and press it flat from the wrong side so the coil lies away from the tape.

3. Place the zipper face down on the fabric right side, with the coil along the seamline and the zipper tape in the seam allowance. Pin in place and hand baste if desired. Using the chosen foot, lower the needle immediately beside the zipper coil. As you lower the presser foot, flatten the coil with the side of a seam ripper or large needle. As you begin to sew, the coil will automatically unfold. Stitch next to the coil but not on top of it, as this will keep the zipper from opening and closing. Stitch from the upper to the lower edge.

4. Repeat to sew the other zipper side to the remaining garment piece, matching the upper raw edges and garment markings across the zipper. Close the zipper.

5. To finish the seam below the zipper, pin the garment right sides together along the seamline. Using a conventional zipper foot, lower the needle into the fabric/zipper tape exactly where the zipper stitching stops. Without backstitching, begin sewing (you may need to use the hand wheel), while gently pulling the zipper tape away from the seam to keep it free of the stitches. Sew the seam, pull the thread ends through to one side of the seam, and tie them. The result should be a smooth seam with no puckers where the zipper ends.

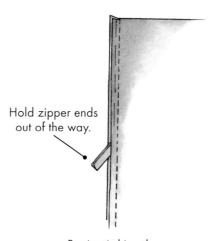

Hold zipper ends out of the way.

Begin stitching the seam at the zipper's lower edge.

Garment side          Seam-allowance side

Sew close to the invisible zipper coil.

# BUTTONS AND BUTTONHOLES

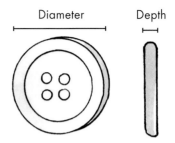

the strip from the fold to the pinch mark and add ⅛" to determine the buttonhole length.

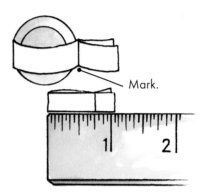

Diameter + depth + ⅛" = buttonhole length

Wrap a paper strip around a shaped button; add ⅛" to its length for buttonhole size.

A button and buttonhole can be used to close any type of overlapped edge. This popular closure is a good choice for any area that will experience pulling or straining, such as garment center fronts and backs, waistbands, or tab-top curtains. In addition to their functional aspects, buttons and buttonholes, used separately or together, can also be used for decorative purposes.

Home-sewing patterns recommend a button size and buttonhole length. If you're using a button size other than the one recommended on the pattern envelope, you'll need to adjust the buttonhole length. You may also need to adjust the pattern to accommodate a larger button, so the buttons don't hang off the garment edge or look too big for the project.

To determine the proper buttonhole length, measure the button's diameter and depth. Add these two measurements together and add ⅛" to allow for the finished buttonhole ends. For ball and oddly shaped buttons, cut a ¼"-wide paper strip and wrap it around the button. Pinch mark where the strip meets at the side edge. Holding the strip ends together, slide the paper off the button and flatten the loop. Measure

## MAKING A BUTTONHOLE

Machine-stitched buttonholes are the easiest to make and can be successfully executed on most fabrics. Most machines have a built-in stitch or special attachment for stitching buttonholes, but any machine with an adjustable-width zigzag stitch can perform the task. Make the buttonholes before attaching the buttons. For most projects, making the buttonholes and sewing on the buttons are the final steps.

1. Make a sample buttonhole on a scrap of the project fabric. Use the same interfacing, thread, and number of fabric layers that will be used in the actual buttonhole. Use this test buttonhole to make sure the button will pass easily, but not loosely, through the buttonhole.

2. Refer to the pattern to mark the buttonhole placement on the fabric right side. For clothing, try on the garment and be sure the button and buttonhole placements are in the desired locations; adjust them if necessary.

3. If the buttonhole area hasn't already been interfaced, cut rectangles of lightweight fusible interfacing about 1" wider and longer than the buttonhole. Center and fuse an interfacing rectangle to the fabric wrong side at each buttonhole location. Position the interfacing so the least amount of stretch is parallel to the buttonhole.

4. Follow the instructions in your sewing-machine manual to stitch the buttonhole using the placement markings from the pattern. Start and stop stitching at the end of the buttonhole that's nearest the project finished edge.

5. Pull the threads to the wrong side and knot the ends. Apply seam sealant to the knot and along the buttonhole center and allow the seam sealant to dry. Alternatively, secure the zigzag stitches by taking three or four small straight stitches along one side of the buttonhole before cutting the threads.

6. Insert a straight pin across each end of a buttonhole. Insert the point of small scissors or a seam ripper into the buttonhole center and cut toward each end. The pins prevent accidentally cutting through the bar tacks and fabric at the buttonhole ends. A chisel-like buttonhole cutter and block can also be used to cut open the buttonholes.

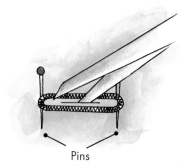

Pins

Beginning at the center, cut toward each end to open the buttonhole.

## SEWING ON A BUTTON

Knowing how to sew on a button will keep you from paying and waiting for someone else to do it, and it's a handy skill to have during fashion emergencies.

There are two basic types of buttons: sew-through and shank. Sew-through buttons have two or four holes drilled through them and can be sewn on by hand or machine. If you're sewing on just one button, it's just as fast to sew it on by hand; but if you have multiple buttons to attach, use the machine to speed up the task.

Sew-through buttons used for decorative purposes can be sewn flat against the fabric, but functional sew-through buttons, used in conjunction with a buttonhole, should be attached with a thread shank. The shank leaves room for the overlap's fabric layers to fit under the button without pulling or distorting the fabric. Shank buttons have a metal or plastic loop that takes the place of a thread shank. These buttons must be attached by hand.

Shank buttons come with a metal or plastic loop on the wrong side to allow room for the buttonhole and fabric layers.

### Button Placement

1. Stitch and cut open the buttonhole(s) as previously described.

2. Lay the garment area with the buttonhole over the corresponding underlap, aligning the appropriate pattern markings. For example, if you're making a button-front blouse, align the center-front markings.

3. For horizontal buttonholes, insert a straight pin though the buttonhole ⅛" from the end closest to the finished edge. Lift the overlap and mark the point where the pin entered the underlap; this will

be along the center front or other matching line. For vertical buttonholes, insert the pin ⅛" from the upper bar tack.

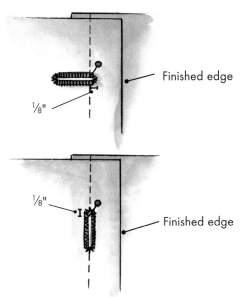

Use completed buttonholes to mark button placements.

4. Place two-hole and shank buttons so the shank or holes are parallel to the buttonhole.

## Hand-Stitched Sew-Through Buttons

1. Mark the button position on the project right side as described in "Button Placement."

2. Cut approximately 18" of thread and run it through beeswax to help strengthen it and prevent tangles. Thread the needle and knot the ends together to create a double strand.

3. Take a small backstitch at the marked button position on the fabric right side. Trim the thread tails close to the knot.

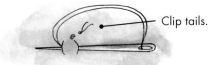

Start button attachment with a small backstitch to secure the thread.

4. Working from the back of the button to the front, insert the needle through one hole. Center the button over the marked button position. Insert the needle through another hole in the button, and then through the fabric.

5. Slip a toothpick or sewing-machine needle between the thread and button. Take three or four more stitches through each pair of holes, ending with the needle and thread on the project wrong side.

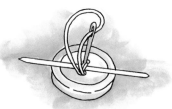

Slip a toothpick or machine needle under the threads.

6. Bring the needle and thread to the right side under the button. Remove the toothpick or needle. Gently pull up on the button so the slack thread is between the button and the fabric. Wrap the threads under the button several times with the needle thread to form a shank. On the final wrap, insert the needle through the loop to create a knot. For additional security, insert the needle and thread through the shank, clip the threads close to the shank, and dot the thread ends with seam sealant. If you prefer, take a small stitch into the fabric, tie a knot, and clip the thread close to the knot.

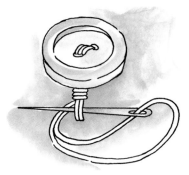

Wrap the threads to form a shank; slip the needle through the loops to tie off.

## Machine-Stitched Sew-Through Buttons

1. Mark the button position on the project right side as described in "Button Placement."

2. Using a glue stick, dab a small amount of glue on the back of the button. Center and press it into place and let the glue dry. Some button-sewing feet have a clamp to hold the button in place, making the glue unnecessary.

3. If your sewing machine has a button-sewing stitch, select it. If it doesn't, set the stitch length to 0 and lower the feed dogs.

4. Attach the button-sewing foot and adjust the stitch width to span the holes in the button. If the presser foot doesn't have an adjustable shank guide, insert a machine needle into the groove on the button foot, centered between the button's holes. Use the hand wheel to move the needle through one complete zigzag cycle, manually checking that the needle swing will not hit the button, needle, or foot.

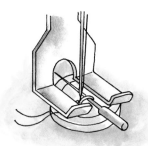

Use a button-sewing foot to attach buttons by machine.

5. Take several stitches to secure the button; then lock the stitches by turning the stitch width to 0 and sewing several stitches in the same buttonhole. Your machine may perform this automatically with its auto-backtack function.

6. Lift the presser foot and remove the needle under the stitches. Without cutting the thread, move to the next button position and repeat the process.

7. When all of the buttons are sewn on, cut the threads halfway between the buttons. Thread the ends through the buttons' holes and wrap them around the slack threads (between the button and the fabric) to form a shank. Tie the ends in a knot, and clip the ends close to the shank. Dot the knot with seam sealant.

Wrap thread tails around the shank threads and tie off.

## SHANK BUTTONS

1. Mark the button position on the project right side as described in "Button Placement." Refer to "Hand-Stitched Sew-Through Buttons" to prepare the needle and thread; take a stitch at the placement mark.

2. Center the button shank over the placement mark with the shank parallel to the buttonhole. Insert the needle through the shank and into the fabric three to four times, ending with the needle on the fabric right side.

Sewing on a shank button.

3. Take several small stitches under the button or knot the thread ends to secure the stitches. Dot the knot with seam sealant.

# CLOSURES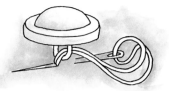

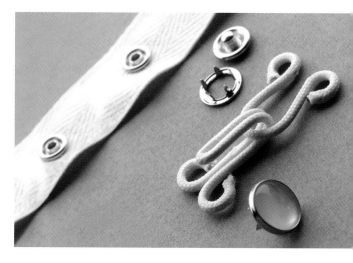

In the previous chapter we talked about buttons, but there are other closure options to choose from. When it comes to finishing a garment or decorative project, choosing the right closure can make the difference between a professional or homemade look. With the array of fasteners on the market, choosing the one that works best for your project and knowing how to apply it is a snap.

## SNAPS

These sturdy closures are often used on children's clothing, men's shirts, outerwear, and at cuff openings. There are three basic types of snaps: sew on, covered, and no sew.

Sew-on snaps have two basic components: a ball, or insertion, piece (male) and a socket, or receiving, piece (female).

Covered snaps are just that: sew-on snaps that have been covered with fabric to coordinate with a project. They come pre-covered in neutral colors, or you can cover them yourself.

## ATTACHING COVERED AND SEW-ON SNAPS

1. Finish the area where the snap will be inserted.

2. Carefully measure each snap's placement, marking where the center of the snap will be positioned with an air- or water-soluble marker. The socket half of each snap should be placed on the right side of the underlapping layer; the ball half should be on the underside of the overlapping layer.

3. Working from the wrong side at the mark, push a pin through the fabric at the mark, and then through the snap part. Position the snap against the fabric; remove the pin. Using coordinating thread, take a few whipstitches through each opening around the snap edge to secure it.

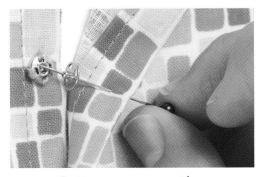

Position sew-on snaps with a pin through the middle hole.

4. Repeat until each snap component is secured. On the overlap, catch only the lower fabric layer so the stitching isn't visible on the garment right side.

## APPLYING A NO-SEW SNAP

No-sew snaps have four components: the ball and socket pieces, and two additional rings with prongs that hold both the ball and socket pieces in place. The rings may be identical, or one may have a decorative stud designed to appear on the garment exterior.

The four components of a no-sew-snap closure

1. Finish the area where the snap will be inserted. For stability, the snap must be inserted through at least two fabric layers or one layer of thick or interfaced fabric.

2. On the fabric-overlap wrong side, use a fabric-marking pen to mark each snap's position.

3. Place the decorative prong piece point side up on a padded surface. Push a pin from the fabric wrong side to the right side at the mark. Align the prong ring center with the pin. Push the fabric, right side down, firmly onto the prongs until the fabric touches the ring base and remove the pin.

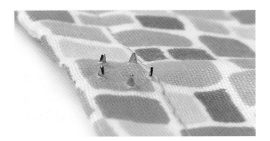

Insert the prong piece from the underlap's wrong side.

4. On the fabric wrong side, place the socket portion of the snap over the prongs with the raised center up. Center a hard-plastic thread spool over the socket and tap it with a hammer or rubber mallet until the prongs are secured in the socket piece, with the fabric firmly sandwiched between the snap segments.

5. On the fabric-underlap right side, precisely measure and mark the center location of the ball (male) snap section. Push a pin to the fabric wrong side at the mark.

6. Align the second prong-piece center with the pin and push the prongs through from the wrong side to the right side. Center the ball section over the prongs and use the same spool and hammer method to secure the prongs. Repeat steps 2–6 until all the snaps are inserted.

Place a spool over the snap and hit it with a hammer to set the snap.

## SNAP TAPE

If sewing or inserting snaps is too daunting or time-consuming for your taste, use snap tape instead. Using snap tape is faster because you don't have to mark and install each snap.

Snap tape consists of a ¾"-wide cotton band with pre-inserted snaps, commonly placed 1½" apart. Separate the ball and socket tapes; stitch along each tape's lengthwise edges to secure it to the fabric. Be sure to align the snaps across the opening and use a zipper foot to avoid hitting the snaps as you sew. For added security and stability, stitch across the tape width ¼" from each snap on both sides.

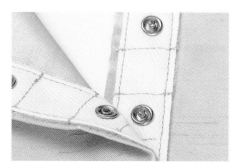

Stitch along the edges to apply snap tape, and across the tape for extra security.

## HOOKS AND EYES

Hook-and-eye closures work well to fasten edges that meet or overlap. They're usually applied at a single point, but they can be used to close an entire opening.

There are two basic types of hook-and-eye closures: general purpose and special purpose. General-purpose hooks and eyes can be used for edges that meet or overlap. They range in size from fine (size 0) to heavy (size 3) and are available in nickel or black finishes and some colors. The general-purpose hook shape is paired with either a straight or a round eye. Straight eyes are used on lapped edges; round eyes are used for edges that meet or abut.

Special-purpose hooks and eyes are usually heavier and larger than general-purpose hooks and eyes. Covered hooks and eyes used on fur garments and jackets fall into this category, as well as the flat hook-and-eye sets made specifically for waistband closures.

### Edges that Meet

Use a hook and round eye and sew both parts to the project wrong side through only one fabric layer. No stitches should be visible on the project right side.

1. Position the hook end about ¹⁄₁₆" in from the garment edge. Whipstitch around each circular opening at the opposite end of the hook, and then slide the needle through the fabric layers and come up at the hook end. Take three or four stitches across the bend of the hook, covering the wire lying flat against the fabric only, to hold the hook in place against the fabric. Secure the threads.

2. Position the eye on the opposite side of the opening so the loop extends about ⅛" beyond the finished edge; the garment edges should just meet when the hook and eye are joined. Whipstitch around each loop and across the bars, and then secure the threads.

Using a hook and eye closure at the top of a zipper tidies the upper edge and adds security to the closure.

## Edges that Overlap

1. Use a hook and straight eye. Position the hook on the overlap wrong side so the hook end is about ⅛" inside the edge. Whipstitch around the circular openings; slide the needle through the fabric layers to surface at the hook end. Take three or four stitches across the bend of the hook, covering the wires lying flat against the fabric only, to hold the hook in place. Secure the threads. The stitches should not be visible on the garment right side.

2. Overlap the edges. Push a pin through the fabric layers at the end of the hook. Mark the right side of the underlap where the pin enters the fabric.

3. Center the eye vertically on the marked spot. Whipstitch around the eyelet at each end; secure the threads.

Attach a hook to the wrong side of the overlap and an eye to the right side of the underlap.

## HOOK-AND-EYE TAPE

For faster hook-and-eye application, use hook-and-eye tape. It functions the same way as snap tape, but with a centered opening instead of lapped edges. For extra stability, stitch around each hook and eye as shown. Stitch the tape to the folded-under layer or facing before construction is complete so the stitching won't be visible on the project right side.

When applying hook-and-eye tape, stitch around each hook and eye individually.

### Making a Thread Eye

Sometimes a buttonhole-stitch eye made entirely of thread is used instead of a metal eye. Thread eyes can be matched to the fabric for a less noticeable finish, and when properly stitched they may be more durable than metal eyes in high-stress areas. Work with single or doubled thread, depending on the thread's size and durability.

To construct a thread eye:

1. Bring the thread to the fabric right side at one end of the eye location and secure it with tiny backstitches. Re-enter the fabric about ¼" away, at the other end of the eye location. Repeat to make a loop of four to six strands; then bring the needle to the fabric right side at the original location.

2. Work closely spaced buttonhole stitches around the thread loops from one end to the other.

3. When the entire loop is covered, take the needle to the wrong side at the end of the eye and knot the thread securely.

## HOOK-AND-LOOP TAPE

Hook-and-loop tape can be used for almost any overlapping closure. It can also be substituted for snaps, hooks and eyes, and buttons. This versatile closure has a soft-looped receiving side and a bristly, hooked fastening side. The tape comes in various colors and widths, but is usually ¾" wide. It's sold by the inch and as short strips, squares, or dots.

Although hook-and-loop tape can be either sew-in or self-adhesive, sew-in is recommended, as it provides greater stability and won't peel away from fabric with wear. Do not attempt to sew through adhesive tapes (unless they're marked as temporary or basting adhesive), as the permanent adhesive will gum the machine needle and cause thread breaks.

To attach hook-and-loop tape:

1. Finish the seam or edges where the hook-and-loop tape will be used. The edges should overlap at least ½" more than the tape width.

2. On the underlap, measure from ¼" below the upper edge to ¼" above the lower edge. Cut a length of hook-and-loop tape to that measurement and separate its halves.

3. On the underlap right side, align the looped portion of the tape ¼" from the upper edge and ¼" in from the long opening edge; pin in place.

4. Match the bobbin thread to the garment fabric. With the hook-and-loop tape on top, secure the closure by edgestitching all four sides.

Hook-and-loop tape makes a secure closure.

5. Repeat this method to apply the hook side to the overlap wrong side. Remember to unfold the fabric enough to allow stitching through the facing only, or use the attachment stitches as decorative topstitching to keep the project right side tidy. Join the hook-and-loop sections to close.

6. To attach hook-and-loop squares or dots, carefully measure and mark the placement of both the hook and loop portions. Center the square or dot on the mark (the loop piece on the underlap right side and the hook piece on the underside of the overlap). Secure by stitching around all four sides or, if the dot is small, use two machine bartacks to hold the dot in place.

# COVERING A BUTTON

A covered button makes for a clean, polished look that coordinates with the project. Use a conventional button-covering kit, or cover your own button with these simple techniques.

## Using a Covered-Button Kit

A covered-button kit includes the following pieces: holder, button shell, button back, and a metal or plastic pusher. The button shell and back can be either metal or nylon and come in a variety of sizes.

The components of a covered-button kit

1. Cut a fabric circle twice the diameter of the button; there's usually a pattern on the packaging. Center the fabric right side down on the indented side of the holder.

2. Gently center the convex side of the button shell on the fabric and press it into the holder. Tuck the extra fabric inside the shell's back.

3. Place a button back, shank side up, over the tucked-in fabric, making sure all the raw fabric edges are concealed. Use the pusher to snap the back securely into the shell.

## Covering a Standard Button

1. Cut a fabric circle twice the diameter of the button. With a needle and a single thread, sew tiny running stitches along the fabric edge.

Sew tiny running stitches around the fabric circle.

2. Center the button on the fabric and pull the thread ends to gather the raw edges, encasing the button.

3. Sew several stitches through the gathered fabric as close as possible to the button. Secure the thread end and trim any excess fabric.

# PATCH POCKETS

As the name suggests, a patch pocket is attached to the fabric surface like a patch. This pocket can be functional or decorative and can be added to a variety of projects, such as totes, garments, or curtains.

## POCKET WITH SQUARE CORNERS

1. Cut out the pocket using the provided pattern, or cut it the size indicated in the instructions. Transfer any markings, such as foldlines and seamlines, from the pattern to the wrong side of the pocket.

2. Finish the upper edge by folding ¼" to the wrong side and pressing; stitch close to the raw edge.

Finish upper edge.

3. Fold the upper pocket edge to the right side along the foldline; pin in place. Stitch the sides of the fold, backstitching at the beginning and end of each seam. Trim the corners to reduce bulk. Turn the pocket facing to the wrong side and press the fold.

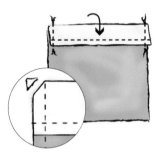

Stitch sides; trim corners.

4. On the wrong side, fold the lower edge to the wrong side on the seamline; press. Fold in the side edges on the seamlines; press. Working from the right side, edgestitch the facing.

Fold in side and lower edges; edgestitch facing.

5. Position the pocket on the project. Edgestitch the pocket in place around the side and bottom edges. Use short stitches and sew close to the folded edge. Reinforce the upper corners with straight or triangular stitching; the triangle will provide more reinforcement for a pocket that will be used often. Pull the thread ends to the wrong side, tie off, and trim.

Stitch pocket in place; reinforce upper corners.

# POCKET WITH ROUND CORNERS

The biggest challenge when making this type of pocket is making the curves identical. The secret is to create a template for perfectly symmetrical pockets every time.

## Making the Template

1. Cut out the pocket pattern on the cutting lines.

2. Cut two 8½" x 11" rectangles from freezer paper. Freezer paper can be used in a copy machine or computer printer to make an accurate template. Be sure the freezer paper isn't curled—it could jam in the printer. Using a scanner or copier, copy the pocket pattern onto the dull side of one piece of the freezer paper.

3. To make the template more sturdy, fuse the copy to the second sheet of freezer paper, positioning the shiny side of the copy against the dull side of the second sheet. Use a Teflon pressing sheet to keep the freezer paper from sticking to your iron or ironing board. Cut out the template along the stitching lines and foldline, removing the seam and hem allowances. If you don't have a scanner or copier, trace the foldline and stitching lines from the pocket pattern onto two fused sheets of freezer paper or one sheet of heavy paper such as card stock and cut out the template.

## Making the Pocket

1. Cut out the pocket using the original pattern, transferring the markings for the foldline and seamlines. Finish each pocket's upper edge by folding ¼" to the wrong side, pressing, and stitching close to the raw edge.

2. Baste ¼" from the curved edges to ease in the fullness. Begin sewing 1" before one curve and continue around to the opposite side, ending 1" past the second curve.

Baste lower edge.

3. Position the template on the fabric, wrong sides together and aligning the template edges with the seamlines; press. The freezer paper should adhere to the pocket fabric.

4. Fold the upper pocket edge to the right side along the foldline; pin in place. With the paper facing up, sew the sides of the facing along the edges of the freezer paper. Trim the corners to reduce bulk. Keeping the pocket template in position, turn and fold the pocket facing to the wrong side, over the template. Press the fold.

5. Using the template as a guide, pull the basting stitches to ease in the corner curves. Press the pocket thoroughly to hold the turned edge. Remove the template.

Pull basting stitches to ease rounded corners.

6. Working from the right side, edgestitch the facing.

7. Position the pocket on the project. Edgestitch the pocket in place around the side and lower edges. Use short stitches and sew close to the folded edge. Reinforce the upper corners with straight or triangular stitching. Pull the thread ends to the wrong side, tie off, and trim.

# TUBE TURNING

Tubes cut on the straight of grain are prone to jamming, especially when too much fabric is pushed toward the turning point. To eliminate this problem, pull the gathers away from the turning point to relieve the jam, and then resume turning. Pull the fabric a little at a time, working around the perimeter of the turning point.

Too much fabric at turning point causes jamming.

Bias tubes are turned more easily because the fabric relaxes and flares at the turning point. However, bias tubes stretch, sometimes resulting in a narrower tube than intended. To minimize narrowing, cut a bias strip with seam allowances that are at least 1" wide. Fold the fabric in half lengthwise with right sides together. Use a short stitch length and stretch the fabric while stitching. Guide the folded fabric edge along the machine markings for the desired tube width rather than guiding along the cut edges. Trim the seam allowances so they're slightly narrower than the desired tube width, and then turn.

## NO-TURN METHOD

If the desired finished tube is at least 1" wide, you can avoid turning it, especially if you plan to edgestitch the tube to finish.

1. Fold under the seam allowances of the short ends and press. Fold and press the strip in half lengthwise with wrong sides together; open the strip. Turn in and press the seam allowances on the long edges; often the seam allowances are wide enough to meet at the center crease and act as self interfacing. Refold the strip with wrong sides together.

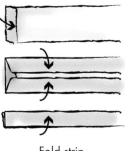

Fold strip.

Straps made of fabric tubes are a popular fashion detail. Find them on casual tank tops as well as bridal and formal wear. It's easy to cut and sew the tubes; the tricky part is turning them right side out without going crazy. But with the right methods and tools, turning tubes can be a breeze.

## TURNING A FABRIC TUBE

The simplest method of tube turning is to use a safety pin as a sort of handle for manipulating the fabric.

1. Sew the tube with right sides together.

2. Pin a large safety pin at one end of the tube. Pinning through the seam allowances gives the pin more bite and may prevent it tearing through the fabric.

3. Push the safety pin into the center of the tube and work it through the tunnel of fabric with your fingers, pulling the attached end along, until you can grasp the safety pin and fabric at the far end of the tube and finish turning it right side out.

2. Edgestitch across one short end, through all layers. Pivot at the corner and continue edgestitching along the strip length. Continue stitching and pivoting around the remaining edges of the strip.

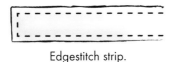

Edgestitch strip.

## TUBE-TURNING PRODUCTS

Tube-turning tools of several types are widely available. Whichever tool you use, work it through the fabric tube as quickly as possible, even if it means temporarily bunching the fabric; as soon as the turned end of the tube emerges from the opposite end, firmly grasp the turned fabric and pull to finish turning the tube right side out. This takes the stress off the tool, which could break loose or damage the fabric. Read the manufacturer's instructions and adjust the cutting dimensions and/or seam allowance of a project to fit the specific tool, if necessary. Test a small sample, following the manufacturer's recommendations, making any adjustments necessary for the fabric weight or texture.

One option, the Fasturn, is a set of rigid tubes that are designed for specific fabric tube diameters. The tool is inserted into the tube, and then a long hook grabs the fabric and pulls it through the metal tube's open center, turning the fabric right side out.

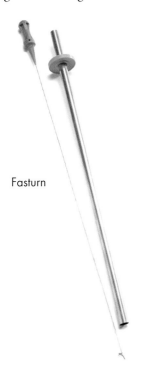

Fasturn

Another possibility is a bodkin, or using a double-eye transfer needle or large blunt tapestry needle as a bodkin. Stitch the tube's lengthwise seam and leave long thread tails—don't cut off the threads. Insert the bodkin partially into the fabric tube. Run the thread tails through the eye of a needle small enough to pass through the eye of the bodkin and use the smaller needle to sew the fabric to the bodkin, passing through both fabric and bodkin several times for strength. Knot the thread tails securely. Work the bodkin through the tube, turning the tube right side out.

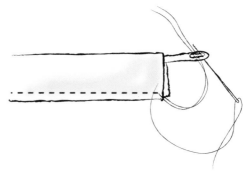

Attach long thread to blunt needle.

Knitting needles or small dowels are useful tools for turning tubes. Stitch across one short end of the strip as well as the long edge. Use a knitting needle or dowel to gently push the tube's closed end through the tube. Do not use any device with a sharp point that would pierce the fabric; when using a knitting needle, push with the blunt, button-like end.

Use knitting needle to turn tube.

Waste cord can also be used to turn a tube right side out. Cut narrow cord (or strong ribbon) at least 2" longer than the tube. On the fabric right side, securely sew the cord to the center of one end. Fold the fabric in half lengthwise, with right sides together, encasing the cord. Taper the seam at the beginning to form a funnel, and then stitch the remainder of the lengthwise seam, taking care not to catch the cord. To turn, simply pull on the cord at the non-stitched end as you pull the fabric in the opposite direction. Trim the funnel end and cord from the turned tube.

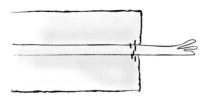

Securely attach cord to one end.

Stitch tube with funnel at end cord is attached to.

## CLOSING ARGUMENTS

If the tube ends will be caught in seams, there's no need to finish the ends. However, if one or both of the ends will be free, the end must be finished to eliminate raw edges.

1. Fold the seam allowances at the open end to the wrong side (inside the tube) and press.

2. Flatten the tube and, holding the pressed edges together firmly between your fingers, whipstitch the opening closed.

3. Optional: Knot the tube ends after finishing.

### Waste Not, Want Not

If you're turning several tubes with waste cord or ribbon, reuse the same length for each tube.

# PIPING

Piping is narrow folded fabric or cording inserted into a seamline for decorative purposes. Divide and conquer could be the philosophy of piping—it divides garments into visible sections and highlights the seaming. Piping defines edges and adds a tailored look, but it also serves a functional purpose by adding stability to edges and corners. In areas where prints or colors of adjacent fabrics can't be matched perfectly, piping creates a deliberate division so the mismatch is less obvious.

The terms *piping, cording,* and *welting* are often used interchangeably, depending on the sewing resource. However, they aren't the same.

**Piping** refers to folded fabric or trim inserted into a seamline and includes a number of variations. Fabric piping may be flat or filled with small, round cording. Novelty piping may be knitted, braided, or twisted. Piping has a flat lip that's inserted into the project seam. The lip may be extensions of the covering fabric, or it may be constructed separately, and then joined to the piping.

Piping lip

Piping has a flat lip that's inserted into the seam.

**Cording** is the filler used inside fabric piping, but the term can also refer to a knitted or twisted trim attached to twill tape or a fabric strip (called a lip). The lip is caught in the seam, leaving the trim exposed at the edge.

**Welting** is the term most often used for home-decor piping, which has a larger diameter than normally found in a garment.

## PIPING OPTIONS

Many types of ready-made piping are available either by the yard or in prepackaged lengths. Fabric-covered piping comes in basic colors; the fabric is usually cotton or a cotton/polyester blend. Look for prepackaged piping in the notions department, and check seasonally for prints, stripes, metallics, or special color groupings.

Finished piping is also available by the yard in many sizes, colors, prints, and fabrics. Check the apparel-trim section at the fabric store, and then venture to the home-decor department for more options.

Look for piping made from twisted cords, round cords, yarns, loops, and woven trims, in addition to the more traditional fabric-covered versions.

## CUSTOM PIPING

When you make your own piping, you can make it in any size, color, and fabric you choose, depending on the project.

What you use for filler determines the size, look, and flexibility of the finished piping. Virtually anything linear is fair game for filler—from string (often used for baby-sized piping) to large-diameter roping (often used for home-decor applications).

Do not use yarn as filler, because it shifts inside the fabric casing. Not all piping has filler—create flat piping by folding the fabric strip in half and eliminating the filler cord.

The most common piping filler is cording, made of either twisted cotton or smooth synthetics in a variety of sizes from ¹⁄₁₆" to 1" in diameter. Rattail—a favorite of many designers—is a smooth synthetic cording that works well for small piping.

Cover piping with fabric to match or contrast with your project, depending on how prominent you want the piping to be. Options for covering piping include using the project fabric right side; using the project fabric wrong side for the same color with a different shade and texture; or using an entirely different fabric, either similar in character or as a contrasting accent, such as stripes, prints, suede, leather, metallic, etc. Many fabric designers offer coordinates within a line that are perfect for go-together piping with slightly different patterning.

## CONSTRUCTION

Depending on the application, piping fabric can be cut on the bias or on the straight grain. Bias-cut fabric offers the most flexibility (literally) for corners and curves, but straight-grain fabric is fine for linear applications. The grain choice will affect the piping appearance if the fabric is patterned or has a prominent weave. Use the fabric's pattern or weave to create a decorative accent, such as varying the look of stripes by cutting them on the bias.

To cover cording for piping, determine the fabric strip width by measuring the cording or filler circumference and adding twice the seam-allowance width to that measurement. To make flat piping, cut fabric strips twice the desired finished width of the piping plus the seam allowances.

## MAKING PIPING FROM BIAS FABRIC STRIPS

1. Cut the fabric strips on the true bias—at a 45° angle to the selvage.

2. Using a clear ruler, a rotary cutter, and a cutting mat, cut parallel fabric strips across the fabric, creating enough length for the finished project's piping, plus seam allowances to join the strips. The resulting short ends will be at a 45° angle.

Cut strips for piping on the true bias.

3. To seam the bias strips, place the short ends right sides together, offsetting the strips so the seamlines, not the corners, match. Stitch using a ¼" seam allowance. Press the seam allowances open. Continue adding strips until you achieve the needed length.

Use diagonal seams to reduce bulk where strips join.

4. Trim off the seam-allowance points for a smooth, straight edge.

Trim the seam-allowance points; press seam allowances open.

## The Skinny on Angled Seams
A diagonal seam is less noticeable and bulky than a seam that runs straight across the strip because the seam-allowance thicknesses are staggered when stitched and finished.

## MAKING PIPING FROM STRAIGHT-GRAIN FABRIC STRIPS

1. Cut either lengthwise or crosswise strips in the determined width.

2. Trim the ends at a 45° angle and seam the strips as detailed for the bias strips.

## MAKING CORDED PIPING

1. Wrap the fabric strip, wrong sides together, around the filler; pin close to the cord.

Wrap fabric strips around the filler cord and pin.

2. Using a zipper foot or a cording/piping foot, adjust the needle position so you can stitch near the cord. Don't stitch right against the cord; any stitching that catches the cord in the seam will tangle the fabric around the cording.

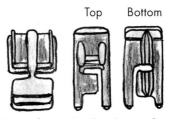

Top          Bottom

Zipper foot    Cording/piping foot

Use a zipper or cording foot.

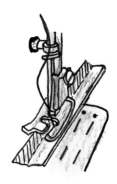

Adjust the foot and/or needle position to stitch near the filler cord.

## Location, Location, Location
If your machine can change the needle position to the right and left, use the needle position to vary the distance between stitching and cord. Sew a little farther away from the cord when basting, and move the needle one or two positions to the left, closer to the cord, for the final stitches.

## APPLICATION

1. Position the piping on the project front, raw edges aligned and right sides together. Baste the piping to the fabric just outside the previous stitching. If your project requires joining pieces with unequal curvature (such as princess seams), stitch the piping to the piece with the most curvature for greater accuracy.

2. Sandwich the piping between project pieces, right sides together. Using the basting line as a stitching guide, stitch the seam just inside the previous stitching. This stitching should lie snugly against the piping so no prior stitching is visible.

### Designer Detail

Piping adds color and texture to a plain fabric, such as the checked fabric shown below. Or use silk ties to cover piping—they're already cut on the bias and offer an interesting fabric accent.

3. It's best if the piping ends in a seamline, but some applications don't allow for that convenience. See "In the Round," opposite, for details.

4. Seam allowances that include piping are generally pressed to one side, rather than pressed open. If the instructions do call for pressing open, turn both piping seam allowances to the side away from the lie of the piping.

5. To eliminate bulk, trim and grade the seam allowances, including the piping, leaving the seam allowances closest to the garment exterior the widest.

6. Continue constructing the project according to the pattern guide sheet.

## CORNERS AND CURVES

Attaching piping around corners and curves requires special handling.

1. To turn a corner, clip the piping seam allowances to, but not through, the stitching line, and ease the piping around the corner; the clipped seam allowances will spread open to fit.

Clip the piping seam allowance at each corner.

2. To attach piping to an outside curve, clip into the piping seam allowances and allow them to spread as they shape to the corner. Ease a little extra piping into the corner so the piping will curve smoothly around the corner when turned to its finished position, without cupping. Be sure to keep both the fabric and the piping flat. If the curve is tight, it may be necessary to notch the seam allowances to reduce bulk in the finished project.

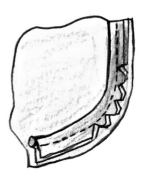

Clip and spread piping seam allowances on outside curves.

**3.** To attach piping to an inside curve, clip into the piping seam allowances if necessary, and allow the clipped seam allowances to overlap slightly, depending on the degree of curvature.

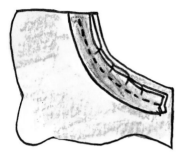

Clip and overlap piping seam allowances on inside curves, or notch the seam allowances.

## IN THE ROUND

Follow this process to join piping ends on a continuous edge, such as a garment hemline or pillow edge.

**1.** Stitch the piping to the project; begin the stitching 1½" from the piping end, placing the end along a straight edge, if possible, and away from converging seamlines to reduce bulk.

**2.** Stitch the piping around the project. As you approach the piping beginning, stop stitching 2" from the starting point and leave the needle down in the fabric. Cut off the piping so it overlaps the original end by 1".

Trim the piping end to overlap the beginning by 1".

**3.** Remove some of the piping basting on both loose ends; trim the filler-cord ends so they abut.

Trim the filler-cord ends so they abut.

**4.** On one piping end, turn ½" of the fabric raw edge to the wrong side, fold it around the other piping end, and continue stitching the piping to the project.

Wrap the turned-under fabric edge over the raw piping end.

Finish stitching the piping to the project.

# BOXING A TOTE

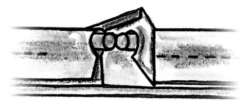

Tote bags are very easy to create; just stitch two fabric rectangles together and add straps. But to give the tote some depth, you can box the lower corners or insert a boxing strip. You can use the same method to shape the corners on a pillow cover to make it boxed rather than knife-edged.

## BOXING CORNERS

Boxing the lower corners on a tote is the quickest way to add dimension.

1. Place the stitched rectangles on a flat surface; finger-press the folds or seamlines at the center bottom and sides.

2. Pick up a lower corner and align the center bottom with its adjacent side seam or crease to form a point.

3. Stitch across the point to form a triangle.

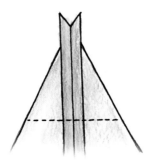

Stitch across the point to form a triangle.

4. Trim the fabric, leaving a ¼" seam allowance beyond the stitching. Zigzag-finish the seam by stitching both raw edges together.

5. Repeat for the second bottom corner.

## BOXING STRIP

A boxing strip is a strip of fabric that's stitched between two fabric rectangles or squares to give a bag more dimension. You can also add a boxing strip to create fuller pillows or cushions.

1. Cut a fabric strip the desired width plus two seam allowances; for this example, use ¼" seam allowances, or ½" total. Cut the strip long enough to span the bag's sides and bottom at the seamline, plus ½".

2. Fold one body piece in half vertically to find the center; pin-mark the lower edge. Fold the boxing strip in half crosswise and mark the center on both long edges.

3. Place the pinned rectangle right side up on your work surface. With right sides together, begin pinning the boxing strip around the rectangle at the lower-edge center. Pin around the corners and along the sides to the upper edge. At each corner, clip the boxing strip almost to the seamline, allowing the seam allowances to spread open as they round the corner.

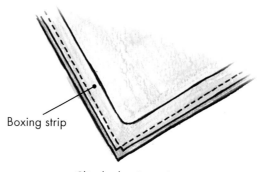

Boxing strip

Clip the boxing-strip seam allowance at each corner.

4. Begin sewing with a ¼" seam allowance at the bag lower-edge center. Stitch to one lower-edge corner until the needle is ¼" from the bag's side edge, at the base of the clip. Leave the needle in the fabric, raise the presser foot, and pivot the fabric. Continue sewing to the upper edge; backstitch. Return to the center bottom and stitch the remaining bag side to the boxing strip, overlapping a few stitches at the center bottom.

5. Repeat to stitch the second bag body to the opposite long edge of the boxing strip.

### Mind the Pins!
Always remove pins as you sew to avoid breaking or damaging your needles.

# DOUBLE-FOLD BINDING

Binding is a strip of fabric that folds over the outside raw edges of a project for a clean and sometimes decorative finish. You'll find it used on quilts, clothing, and home-decor projects. Simple place mats and pot holders are great projects for learning this technique.

1. Measure around all the edges of the project that will be covered by the binding. Divide the total inches by 37 to determine the number of strips to cut. Cut strips 2½" wide (or as directed by the pattern) along the crosswise fabric grain (from selvage to selvage, the width of the fabric).

2. Remove the selvages from the strips. To join the strips, place the ends of two binding strips perpendicular to each other, right sides together; the overlapped area forms a square. Stitch diagonally across the square and trim the seam

allowances to ¼". Join all the strips in this way and press the seam allowances open.

Join binding strips with diagonal seams; trim seam allowances to ¼".

3. Cut the beginning of the binding strip at a 45° angle. Fold the binding strip in half lengthwise with wrong sides together and press. Beginning in the middle of a side and leaving a 6" tail of binding free, align the binding raw edges with the quilt edge.

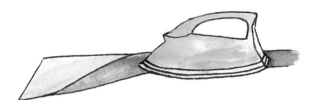

Fold the binding in half and press.

4. Begin sewing the binding to the quilt using a ¼" seam allowance. Stop sewing ¼" from the first corner and backstitch. Remove the needle from the quilt and cut the threads.

5. Rotate the quilt into position for sewing the next side. Fold the binding up at a 45° angle, and then fold the binding back on itself even with the raw edge of the quilt. Begin stitching at the raw edge, backstitch to secure, and continue sewing to a point ¼" from the next corner. Repeat at all corners.

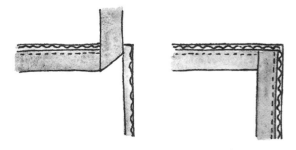

Fold the binding up, and then down to miter the corner.

6. When nearing the starting point, leave at least 12" of the quilt edge unstitched and a 10" to 12" binding tail.

7. Smooth the beginning tail over the ending tail. Following the cut edge of the beginning tail, draw a line on the ending tail at a 45° angle.

Draw a line on the ending tail using the beginning tail as a guide.

8. To add a seam allowance, draw a cutting line ½" beyond the first line; make sure it guides you to cut the binding tail ½" longer than the first line, creating an overlap. Cut the binding end on the second line.

Add ½" for seam allowances.

Cut on the second line, creating a ½" overlap.

9. To join the ends, place them right sides together. Offset the points so the strip edges match at the seamline and sew the seam. Press the seam allowances open. Press the final section of binding in half lengthwise, and then finish sewing it to the quilt.

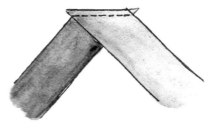

Join the binding ends with a diagonal seam.

Press the binding seam allowances open.

10. If necessary when binding a quilt, trim away the excess backing and batting only in the corners to eliminate bulk. There should be enough seam allowance to fill the binding completely when it's turned over the quilt edge.

11. Fold the binding to the back of the quilt, enclosing the raw edges. Pin the binding in place, just covering the machine stitching. Tuck in the corners to form neat miters on both front and back.

12. Blindstitch the binding to the backing. Stitch the miter folds also, if desired.

Blindstitch the binding to the backing.

A neatly mitered binding is the perfect finish for a quilt.

# WAISTBANDS

An elastic or drawstring waistband is part of every beginning sewist's repertoire, but every fashion-conscious sewist knows that there's more to life–and your wardrobe–than elastic waistbands.

Familiarize yourself with different types of waistbands and construction techniques to help you achieve better fit, comfort, and style. Alter your favorite patterns to include waistbands that suit both the garment and your personal taste.

What makes you reach into your closet for the same pair of pants again and again? Chances are, your favorite pair is comfortable, flatters your figure, and has a waistband that fits perfectly. Perhaps no single element so strongly affects a garment's wearability as a well-constructed waistband that fits—as most of us can attest after a day of enduring one that doesn't.

## ANATOMY OF A WAISTBAND

A waistband is created by one of two methods: either a casing formed from an extension of the garment fabric is folded over into a band and finished; or the band is assembled separately, seamed, and/or contoured, and then stitched to the garment.

When selecting a waistband finish, consider the pant or skirt design, type of fabric, anticipated wear, and personal style. The standard 1¼"-wide, straight-cut waistband is one option available, but most patterns can be altered to accommodate a number of variations.

To prevent stretching, reinforce non-elastic waistbands with interfacing, ribbon, or seam binding. Loosely woven fabrics and wide or contoured waistbands especially need the additional support of interfacing to hold their shape. With knit fabrics, opt for an elasticized waistband.

### Measuring Up

Take your measurements while wearing the undergarments you plan to wear under the finished pants or skirt. Measuring over regular clothing or heavier garments may result in a loose waistband with too much ease.

## ELASTIC CASING WAISTBAND

An elastic waistband is easy to make and comfortable to wear—so it's perfect for pajama pants, lounge pants, or casual skirts. The most basic elastic waistband is made by folding down an extension of the garment fabric to form a casing and inserting the elastic.

1. If your pattern doesn't have an elastic waistband, add 4" above the waistline.

2. Baste the seam allowances open from the raw edge to a point about 4" below the upper edge to keep them flat. This makes it easier to insert the elastic.

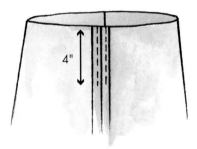

Baste the seam allowances to the garment within the casing area.

3. Zigzag- or serge-finish the garment upper edge. Turn down the casing the amount specified in the pattern (often 2¼", but it will vary with the elastic width) and press the fold. Stitch close to the fold, beginning and ending at a side seam, overlapping the stitching.

4. Stitch along the lower edge of the casing, leaving a 2" opening at one side seam.

Stitch the casing's lower edge,
leaving a 2" opening.

5. Measure your waist and subtract 5" to allow for stretch and a snug fit. Measure the elastic to this length and test it by wrapping it around your waist while you're sitting down; try different amounts of stretch until you're satisfied with the fit, and then cut the elastic this length. Use a safety pin to join the elastic ends and be sure the elastic can stretch around the widest part of your hips; if not, increase the length.

6. Attach a safety pin or bodkin to one end of the elastic and insert it into the casing opening. Pin the opposite end of the elastic to the garment to prevent its being pulled into the casing. Guide the elastic through the casing. Remove the pin and overlap the elastic ends by 1", making sure the elastic isn't twisted in the casing. Zigzag the overlapped ends securely, stitching through both elastic layers.

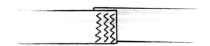

Zigzag the overlapped elastic ends securely.

7. Machine stitch the casing opening closed, connecting the ends of the earlier stitching. Distribute the casing-fabric fullness evenly around the elastic; pin at the side and center-back seams. Stitch in the ditch along the seams, through the elastic and casing, to keep the elastic from rolling and shifting.

Stitch in the ditch at side and back
seamlines to keep the elastic from twisting.

## STRAIGHT WAISTBAND

Classic and versatile, the straight waistband is appropriate for any figure.

1. Cut a straight-grain fabric strip with one long edge along the fabric selvage, making the strip 6" to 8" longer than your actual waistline measurement and twice the desired finished width plus 1¼" for seam allowances (for example, for a 1"-wide finished band cut a 3¼"-wide strip).

2. Apply appropriate interfacing to the strip. Cut the interfacing half as wide as the waistband and trim all but ⅛" of the interfacing from the seam allowances; see "Interfacing" on page 12 for details. Fold the interfaced strip in half crosswise, and mark the raw edge by snipping at the fold to mark the center back (or the right side seam if your pattern has a side zipper). Unfold the waistband and machine baste ⅝" from the long raw edges with a contrasting thread color. Machine baste along the ⅝" waist seamline of the pants or skirt.

3. Before fitting the waistband to the pants or skirt, try on the garment. Be sure you can pinch at least 1" of ease at the waist seamline. Make any adjustments necessary for a proper fit.

4. With right sides together and the center back (or the left side seam) matching the snip mark, pin the waistband raw edge to the pants or skirt waist; pin parallel to the seamline. Wrap the waistband to the wrong side, over the pins, and try on the pants or skirt. The pants/skirt waistline and waistband should be about 1" larger than your waist measurement; ease the pants/skirt waistline slightly to fit the waistband, if necessary. If you've adjusted the pants/skirt waistline, re-pin the band and try on the garment again.

5. When you're satisfied with the fit, trim the excess waistband length, allowing a ⅝" seam allowance at one end and a 2" to 3" overlap/underlap and seam allowance at the other end for a button or hook-and-eye closure. Sew the waistband raw edge to the pants/skirt, and then finish the short ends. When stitching the end at the zipper edge, stitch the short end ¹⁄₁₆" past the overlap edge to allow for turning the band smoothly without bulk. Press the seam allowances toward the waistband.

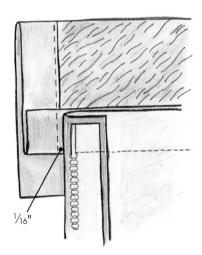

Stitch ¹⁄₁₆" beyond the zipper edge to allow for the fabric thickness when the waistband is turned.

6. Turn the waistband right side out, clipping the waistband seam allowance to the basting stitches just past the zipper tape on each side. Turn under the seam allowances on the overlap/underlap and above the zipper; slip-stitch in place. Position the selvage edge so it extends ⅝" past the waistline stitching; pin in place from the garment right side. Working with the right side up, stitch in the ditch (stitch with the needle in the well of the seam) to catch the waistband selvage edge.

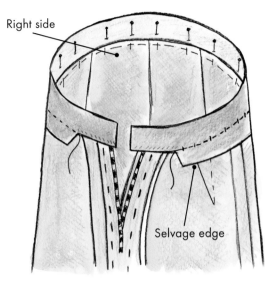

Stitch in the ditch to catch the selvage edge.

## BELT LOOPS

Belt-loop application begins before the waistband is attached to the skirt or pants, so plan ahead to include belt loops.

1. Plan the belt-loop length to equal the belt width plus 1½"; the belt width should be in proportion to the waistband. Cut a fabric strip three times the desired finished-loop width by the total length needed for all the loops plus an inch or two as insurance. Cut the strip with the fabric selvage along one long edge—or zigzag, overcast, or serge one long edge to finish it.

2. Fold and press the strip into thirds with the raw edge enclosed. Topstitch both long edges; be sure to catch the selvage or finished edge in the stitches. Cut the strip into the required number of loops.

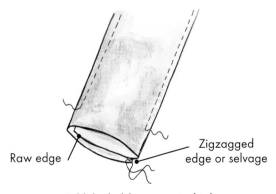

Fold the belt-loop strip in thirds and topstitch both long edges.

3. With right sides together, position the loops along the waist seamline of the garment with raw edges matched; pin or baste in place.

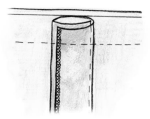

Pin or baste the belt loops to the waist seam.

4. Apply the waistband, catching the loops in the stitching. Finish the waistband.

5. Press the loops up, across the waistband, and turn under ½" at the upper edge of each belt loop. Pin the loops in place along the waistband's upper edge and topstitch through all layers.

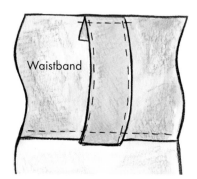

Topstitch the folded belt loop along the waistband's upper edge.

## WAISTBAND STYLES

Straight waistbands sit just above the natural waistline. A folded or faced rectangular band is attached to the garment after other details are complete.

Straight

Faced waistbands allow the finished edge of a skirt or pants to rest at the natural waist with a no-waistband appearance. Finish the waistband with a facing made from lining, lightweight fabric, or grosgrain ribbon to reduce bulk.

Faced

Contoured waistbands rest below the natural waist. Shaped to the curve of the body, this style accommodates size variation from waist to hips. A contoured waistband has shaped pieces that are sewn together first, and then attached to the garment.

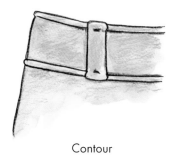

Contour

Elastic waistbands are comfortable and provide give at the waistline. A length of elastic (or a drawstring) is inserted through a casing, cinching the fabric at the waist while allowing the garment to be pulled over the hips. Variations include waistbands that are fitted in front and elasticized in the back and side-elastic waistbands, which offer the look of a tailored waistband in both the front and back while giving elastic ease at the less-noticeable side seams.

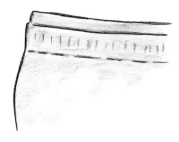

Elastic

## GIRLS VS. BOYS

A few differences between men's and women's waistbands are worth noting. First, overlapping ends of a woman's waistband fasten with the overlap facing the left or back; side closings are placed on the left. The opposite is true of menswear, in which the flap and/or overlap fasteners face right. A men's pants waistband typically includes a center-back seam, making the pants easier to alter. Finally, the upper edge of menswear waistbands (either straight or elastic casing) sits at the waistline, rather than fitting above the natural waistline, as on women's wear.

# SERGING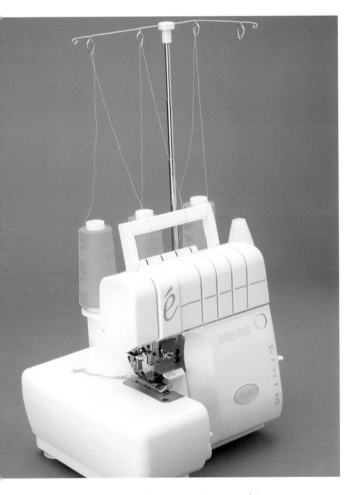

When you purchased your sewing machine, you may have noticed some compact, squarish machines in the store with three, four, five, or even eight spools of thread. These are sergers, and they can make your sewing life much easier.

Like sewing machines, sergers range from the very basic to models with more bells and whistles. In general, the more threads a serger has, the more functions and stitches it can perform—and the more it will cost. Visit dealers in your area and take several models for a test-drive as you decide which machine best fits your budget and desires.

A serger creates finished seams as seen on ready-made garments, such as side seams in sweatshirts and T-shirts. A serger speeds up the sewing process because it can stitch a seam, finish the raw edges, and trim off excess fabric—all in one step. To accomplish the same results using a regular sewing machine would require three separate steps. But a serger isn't a substitute for a regular sewing machine. It can perform a variety of functions and handle many different fabrics, but it can't do everything a sewing machine can, like make buttonholes.

The most basic stitch on a serger is the overlock stitch. A serger has upper and lower loopers to carry the threads that form loops above and below the fabric, binding the edge. The looper threads engage with the needle threads to form an overlock stitch. A three-thread overlock stitch uses one needle thread (one needle thread plus two looper threads). A four-thread overlock stitch uses two needle threads.

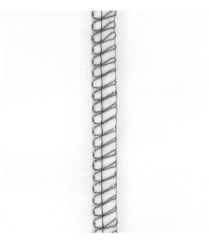

A four-thread overlock stitch

Each thread path on a serger has an individual tension adjustment. This is an advantage, because the ability to adjust each thread's tension separately allows the greatest range of stitch variations and fabric choices.

When the tension is adjusted correctly, you'll see two lines of straight stitching on the top made by the needles, and the upper and lower looper threads will meet perfectly on the edge. On the underside of the fabric, you'll see dots where the needle threads wrap around the lower looper thread. Thread tensions can also be adjusted to create various specialty stitches.

A balanced stitch seen
from right and wrong sides

Standard serger thread is two-ply, which means it's made from two strands twisted together, and comes on a cone. Thread used with standard sewing machines is three-ply. Serger thread is thinner and more lightweight than standard sewing thread to help eliminate bulk at the seamlines. When you become more comfortable and experienced with your serger, experiment with decorative threads in the loopers to create different effects.

As a beginner, you may use a serger mostly for finishing seams. As you become more experienced, you'll use the serger for seaming (you can make entire garments using only a serger), gathering, rolled hems, decorative effects, and more.

When you buy a serger, look for a dealer who offers new-owner classes to learn the basics of your new machine and expand your knowledge of its capabilities. Ongoing support classes are also important as you build your skills. A serger may look intimidating, but with a reputable dealer as your guide you'll be able to thread your serger and learn how to incorporate it into your sewing life.

### Serger Dos & Don'ts

DON'T—Buy your serger, bring it home, and leave it in the box.

DO—Set it up right away. Cut out pajamas, T-shirts, and shorts and get started. The sooner you get comfortable with the serger, the more you'll use it.

Sergers are worth the learning curve—you'll wonder how you ever sewed without one.

DON'T—Put off taking new-owner classes.

DO—Sign up right away for classes. You'll learn so much more, and more quickly, in a class environment than at home. Everyone benefits from things that happen in classes, such as seeing how others' problems are solved and sharing serger experiences with other students.

# SEWING WITH . . .

# SEWING WITH FLEECE

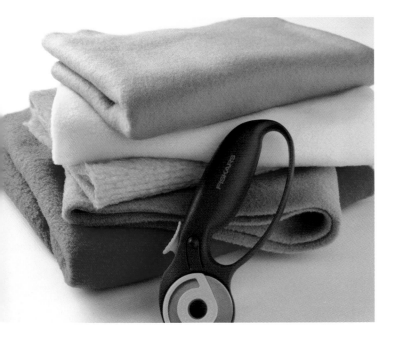

Fleece is a favorite *Sew Simple* fabric, not only because it's easy to sew and super comfy, but also because it's eco-friendly by nature. It's manufactured from recycled bottles—who knew plastic could be so cozy? Fleece comes in a huge array of bright colors and wacky prints, and works great for clothing, home decor, and accessory projects alike. It's a knit fabric, so it's stretchy and generally the edges don't ravel. Fleece is warm without being bulky, and it stands up to lots of washing and drying. Find out how to sew with fleece by following these useful pointers.

## PICK YOUR FLEECE

Fleece comes in numerous weights and types. Some fleece fabrics even have special water-resistant or odor-repellant finishes. Usually, the heavier the fleece, the less drape it has. Heavier fleece is best for outdoor apparel and accessories, whereas lightweight fleece works well for baby clothes or pajamas. Check the recommended fabrics listed on the pattern envelope to make sure that the fleece you want to use is appropriate for the project you're making.

Like velvet or chenille, fleece has a pile. The most common type of fleece resembles felt with its fuzzy, brushed pile. Check out the fleece section of the fabric store to find different types and textures, including fleece that resembles fur or shearling.

Unless fleece fabric has a one-way print, it can be tricky to tell the difference between the right and wrong sides. It doesn't matter too much which side you choose, but one way to determine which is which is to stretch the fabric crosswise. The fabric's cut edges will curl to the wrong side.

## CUT IT OUT

Fleece has a fluffy pile, which means it has a nap. The nap refers to the natural lie of the fibers in the pile; you can easily feel the nap when you run your hand up or down the fabric, as one is smooth and the other rough. When you cut out your pattern pieces, refer to the "with nap" instructions to ensure that the pile runs the same way for every pattern piece.

Because of its bulk, it's best to cut fleece just one layer at a time. For straight, even edges, use a rotary cutter with a new sharp blade in combination with a cutting mat and an acrylic ruler.

## PINS, NEEDLES, AND THREAD

Use long sharp pins on fleece, as short pins tend to become lost in the pile. Another option for holding seams together while you sew is to use basting tape, a narrow double-sided tape that dissolves in water.

For the smoothest possible sewing, use an 80/12 or 90/14 universal, stretch, or ballpoint sewing-machine needle; these needles have rounded tips that are less likely to snag the knit fabric structure. The needle dulls more quickly on fleece than with other fabrics, so you'll need to change it more often to avoid skipped stitches.

Use polyester thread rather than cotton when sewing with fleece. The polyester fiber is stronger and more compatible with the synthetic fabric.

## SEW AHEAD

Before you begin your fleece project, test by sewing on some fleece scraps to determine the most effective tension, stitch length, sewing speed, and so on. Set your machine to a longer stitch length, between 3 and 4 mm. This prevents wavy seams and keeps the stitches from sinking too tightly into the fabric. If your machine has stretch stitches in its menu, consider one of those for sewing on fleece for seams that give with movement.

Use slightly less pressure than usual on the machine presser foot as you sew. A roller or even-feed presser foot is also helpful for guiding the fabric through the machine.

Fleece tends to shed quite a bit during sewing. Clean the fuzz out of your machine often using canned air or a brush.

**Go Easy on the Heat**
Fleece will melt if too much heat is applied. Set your iron on very low heat, or simply finger-press. Use steam to press seam allowances open.

## THE FINISHING TOUCH

Since fleece fabric doesn't ravel, you can leave the cut edges completely raw. Other fun options include trimming the edges with pinking shears for a zigzag effect, or cutting with a wavy or scalloped rotary-cutter blade.

If you prefer to hem the edges, fold the fabric raw edges ½" to the wrong side. Stitch close to the raw edge using a straight stitch or wide zigzag stitch. For a hand-finished look, blanket stitch or whipstitch around the edges.

# SEWING WITH KNITS

Knits are quick to sew and easier to fit than woven fabrics, since knits stretch over body curves. The stretchy quality of knits, however, can make them tricky to work with, requiring some specialized sewing techniques.

## CHOOSING A PATTERN

Patterns designed for knit fabrics are labeled as such on the pattern envelope. You can make knit garments with patterns designed for woven fabrics, but you may need to make a smaller size than the instructions indicate; more wearing ease is built into patterns for woven fabrics since they don't stretch. If you've never sewn with knits, choose a designed-for-knits pattern to avoid frustration and the need for many fitting adjustments.

Knit fabrics have different degrees of stretch. Some stretch very little, while others may stretch to more than twice their original size. Patterns for knitwear have a stretch guide on the envelope, or specify the amount of stretch required. Choose fabric that matches the stretch recommendation so the finished garment will be the right size.

To determine the percentage of fabric stretch, fold the fabric along the crosswise grain in the middle of the fabric; folding along the edge gives an inaccurate reading. Measure and place a pin at each end of a

4" section along the fold. Holding the folded edge at the pins, place one pin at the end of a ruler and pull the fabric with the other hand to see how far it easily stretches. If it stretches to 5", it has 25% stretch; 6" equals 50% stretch; 7" equals 75% stretch, and 8" equals 100% stretch.

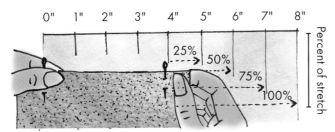

Stretch along a crosswise fold.

While still holding the fold at the zero mark, let the fabric relax and measure it again to check its recovery. It should return to its original size—if it doesn't, the finished garment will sag with wear.

Most knits have less lengthwise stretch than crosswise stretch. The lengthwise stability reduces bagginess at elbows, knees, and seat. The crosswise stretch goes around the body, building in comfort and often eliminating the need for darts and other shaping details.

Ribbing, binding, or turned-and-stitched necklines are frequently substituted for facings in knit garments, and zippers are preferred over button closures. Look for patterns with these design elements, or choose other patterns that can be adapted easily.

## PREPARING THE FABRIC

Prewash knits before cutting not only to minimize shrinkage, but to remove sizing and excess dye, which can build up on the needle and cause skipped stitches. Preshrink the fabric using the same method you'll use to launder the finished garment.

Don't preshrink ribbing unless it's a color that might bleed—such as red. The ribbing will shrink; to maintain its intended elasticity, cut it to size before preshrinking. Gently hand rinse and lay flat to dry. Stretch the ribbing to fit the garment edge when stitching.

## PATTERN LAYOUT

If you can't tell which is the fabric right side, choose one side for the right side and use it consistently throughout the garment construction. Chalk-mark or place a piece of tape on the wrong side of each cut piece to prevent confusion.

Use a with-nap layout for pattern placement. Knits can catch the light differently if cut with the grainline running in different directions, resulting in the appearance of irregular shading.

If a knit runs, it will only run in one direction. Test the fabric by pulling along both crosswise ends. If ladders form at one end, position the pattern pieces so runs start at the lower edge of each garment piece. Fabric at the hemline is less stressed than at the neck or waistline edges.

Correct grainline placement is important. Don't use the fabric edge as a grainline reference; the edge may not be parallel to the vertical columns (wales) of knit stitches. Instead, chalk-mark or thread-trace a line along one of the wales. Place the pattern grainline arrow parallel to the marked line to keep the garment from twisting around the body. The exceptions are knits with a horizontal stripe; when cutting those, position the stripes perpendicular to the grainline and be sure they meet at the edge when the fabric is folded. Don't stretch the fabric to straighten it—if the stripes don't align, it's best to find another fabric.

When using knits containing spandex, perform the stretch test as directed above to see which direction (lengthwise or crosswise) has the greater stretch and place the pattern pieces so the greater stretch goes around the body. Refold the fabric along the crosswise grain to accommodate the pattern pieces if necessary.

If the fabric fold is a permanent crease that pressing won't remove, refold the fabric or use an alternate layout. Don't place a permanent crease along a center front or back where it will detract from the garment's appearance. If the creased area must be used, place it at the vertical center of the sleeves.

Match plaid or striped designs at the seams. When cutting the bodice and sleeves, the design should match at the top of the underarm seam. Trace full patterns for the front and back pieces and cut one fabric layer at a time. For patterns requiring two cut pieces, flip the pattern over for the second piece to be sure you cut right and left sides. Keep stripes level across a pattern piece to avoid a barber-pole effect when worn.

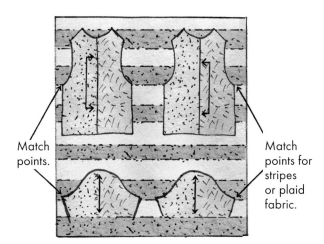

Match points.

Match points for stripes or plaid fabric.

For perfectly matched seams, cut out on single layer and match at underarm seams.

## CUTTING TIPS

Lightweight knits (such as tricot, sheer, or synthetic interlock) slip around when pinning and cutting. To combat this tendency, place newspaper or tissue paper on the cutting table under the fabric and pattern. Pin through all layers to stabilize the fabric, and then cut.

Make sure your cutting tools are sharp; use barber shears or shears with serrated blades. A rotary cutter is another option; cut by pushing away from you, holding down the pattern with your free hand. Always protect the cutting surface with a self-healing mat when using a rotary cutter.

Don't let the fabric hang off the cutting surface; the knit will stretch and distort. Accordion-fold any excess fabric and support it on a table or a chair. Unfold as needed to continue cutting.

When cutting heavyweight knits (such as sweatshirt knits and fleece), trim the pattern along the cutting lines and pin it only to the upper layer of doubled fabric. Cut through both layers, holding the pattern and fabric in place with your free hand. If you cut off the pattern notches, mark their placement with a marking pen at the fabric edge; snipping into the seam allowance weakens the seams.

Use fabric-marking pencils, tailor's chalk, tailor's tacks, or disappearing-ink marking pens to transfer the pattern markings. Don't use a tracing wheel with prongs—it can snag the fabric.

## INTERFACING

Interfacing serves two different purposes when used with knit garments. When used to add body, it must flex with the fabric. When used as a stabilizer, it prevents the fabric from stretching.

In general, choose a knitted interfacing to add body and a nonwoven interfacing to stabilize the stretch. However, a tricot-knit interfacing can also be used to stabilize fabric by turning it so the interfacing's crosswise stretch is perpendicular to the crosswise stretch of the fabric.

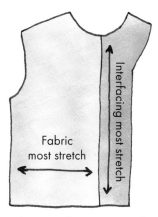

Fabric most stretch

Interfacing most stretch

Place interfacing so stretch directions are opposite one another.

Preshrink interfacing before cutting it. Fold it into a square that will fit in the sink; fill the sink with warm water and let the interfacing soak until the water cools. Squeeze out the water without twisting, and gently roll the interfacing in a towel to remove any excess water. Lay flat or hang over a shower rod to dry. Even fusible interfacings can be preshrunk this way.

## SEAMING

Use a new ball-point, universal, or stretch needle. A worn needle can cause skipped stitches or snag the fabric. If you experience skipped stitches with a universal needle, change to a ball-point needle for heavier fabrics or a stretch needle for finer knits. Use a size 60/8 or 75/11 needle for light- to mediumweight knits and size 80/12 or 90/14 for heavier knits.

Always stitch a test seam. If there are tiny holes along the seamline, the needle is too big, damaged, or sharply pointed and is breaking the fabric thread loops.

Set the machine at 8 to 10 stitches per inch (2.5 to 3 mm). Looser knits may require a longer stitch. Stitches that are too short restrict the fabric recovery and will result in rippling.

Incorporate stretch in the seams so the threads don't break with movement. Test the following different methods to see which works best for the fabric.

- Sew with a straight stitch, gently stretching the fabric in front of and behind the presser foot as you sew.

- Choose a built-in stretch stitch. These stitches automatically add stretch to the seam, so don't stretch the fabric as it's sewn. Be certain the garment is already fitted; stretch stitches are extremely difficult to remove without damaging the fabric.

- Three- and four-thread serger stitches are also good for sewing knits. For even more stretch, use low-twist textured nylon or polyester thread (such as Woolly Nylon) in the needle and loopers.

- A narrow, short zigzag (1 mm long, 1 mm wide) is a strong, yet flexible stitch for T-shirt knits and wool jerseys. Make a test seam and spread it apart—if it "ladders," revealing the threads between the fabric layers, narrow and shorten the stitch. Don't stretch the seam while sewing.

Don't sew over pins—a good reminder for any fabric. Hitting one can damage needles, the serger blade, and possibly your machine. A blunt needle can cause snags, holes, or runs in seams and topstitching.

To control curling fabric edges, use wash-away basting tape or a glue stick within the seam allowances when placing the pieces together for seaming. Allow the glue to dry completely before stitching to avoid gumming the needle. Either of these aids can also help align plaids, stripes, or prints at the seams.

Some knit patterns use ¼" seam allowances; others allow ⅝", so check the pattern instructions before seaming.

Use a double-stitched seam unless the knit has little stretch (like some double knits). Stitch on the seamline and then again ⅛" to ¼" from the first stitching in the seam allowance. If using a straight stitch for both rows,

stretch the seam equally each time. After stitching, carefully trim next to the second row of stitches, leaving a total seam allowance of ¼". A serger can seam and trim in one operation—be sure the needle stitches at the appropriate seamline location.

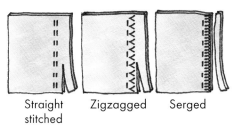

Straight stitched   Zigzagged   Serged

Use double-stitched seams.

Press double-stitched seam allowances toward the garment back. For knits that don't curl at the edges, stitch using a ⅝" seam allowance and press the seam allowances open for a flatter finish, adding extra seam allowance to the pattern pieces if necessary.

Knits don't ravel, so no seam finish is required. Adding a seam finish adds bulk, something to avoid whenever possible while sewing with knits.

### Testing, Testing

When sewing knits, always sew test seams to be sure you have the best combination of needle, stitch type, and thread.

## PRESSING

Pressing knits during construction is just as important as when sewing woven fabrics. Follow these tips for best results.

- Avoid stretching the fabric when pressing. Use an up-and-down motion instead of resting the iron on the fabric and sliding it back and forth. Don't let the garment hang over the edge of the ironing board while it's still warm and moist; gravity will pull the fabric out of shape. Let the fabric rest flat on the ironing board until it has cooled and dried. Synthetic fibers are more susceptible to stretching while warm, so take special care when handling them. Position the ironing board next to a table or counter to help support the fabric when pressing.

- Press as you sew. Never cross a seam, dart, tuck, or pleat with another seam without pressing it first.

- Prevent seam-allowance imprints by using a curved surface like a seam roll or seam stick under the seamline.

- Serged or double-stitched seams should be pressed toward the garment back whenever possible.

- Test a fabric scrap to determine the correct iron temperature. If the fabric is fragile or sensitive to heat, use a press cloth. Try different levels of pressure to see how they affect the fabric. Iron pressure of any kind can permanently distort or flatten some ribbings or sweater knits. Hold the iron above the fabric for steaming; then lightly finger-press the seam.

- Use lots of steam and a clapper to tame stubborn seams on fabrics that can endure the pressure.

## Buttonholes

- Back fabric with interfacing before stitching buttonholes to prevent them from stretching out of shape. Interfacing shouldn't make the fabric stiff; use a fusible tricot or a lightweight, sew-in, woven interfacing and test on a swatch. When using tricot interfacing, rotate it so the crosswise stretch is perpendicular to the fabric's crosswise stretch to minimize stretching. Test-stitch buttonholes on an interfaced fabric scrap before stitching on the garment.

- Buttonholes can "fish mouth" even when the area has been interfaced. Instead of using a satin zigzag stitch, which can ripple, lengthen the stitch slightly so it's less dense.

- To further stabilize the fabric, place water-soluble stabilizer under the fabric. If a lacy knit has openings that might catch on the presser foot or if the knit has a high loft, place a second layer of water-soluble stabilizer on top.

- Stitch buttonholes on ribbed knits parallel to the ribs if possible, allowing the ribbing to stretch uniformly.

## HEMMING

Sew hems on knit garments by hand or machine. Interface the hem with a very lightweight fusible interfacing to keep it from stretching; then turn up the hem and stitch.

Using a stretch twin needle produces an excellent hem with some stretch. Machine stitching on the crosswise fabric grain can ripple the hem, so don't stretch the hem while sewing. A serger cover stitch also gives a nice hem finish.

Topstitched hems are more casual than blindstitched hems. A blind hem catch stitch is an excellent choice if sewing by hand—each stitch is a disconnected backstitch, adding flexibility to the hem.

To machine stitch a blind hem, fold up the hem, and then turn back the garment ⅛" to ¼" (3 to 6 mm) below the hem raw edge. Sew with the majority of stitches on the extended section, barely catching the fold with the left needle swing. For more information, see "Machine-Stitched Hems" on page 19.

Machine stitch a blind hem.

For a serger blind hem, use a three-thread stitch. Set the machine to the longest and widest stitch possible; slightly loosen the needle thread tension. Match the needle thread color to the garment. Turn the hem up and back as for the blind hem above. Serge along the hem upper edge, barely catching the fold with the needle. When the hem is pressed, you'll see tiny picks of thread on the right side.

Stitch a blind hem on a serger.

SEWING WITH KNITS

# SEWING WITH LEATHER

Sewing with leather can be intimidating. Leather is a bit pricey, and needles leave permanent holes. One mistake forcing you to rip out stitches can cause major disappointment. With these 10 simple tips to guide you through the process, you'll sew leather with ease and achieve professional-looking results.

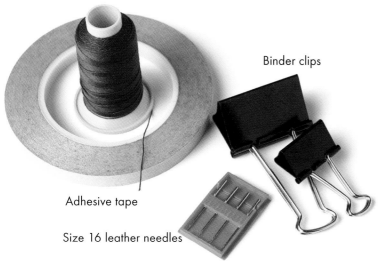

Upholstery thread

Binder clips

Adhesive tape

Size 16 leather needles

Using the right tools will lead to success when working with leather.

1. Consider cutting the project pieces from both interfacing and leather. Fuse the interfacing to the wrong side of the leather using a press cloth and the least amount of heat possible. Interfacing helps the leather retain its shape and facilitates moving it evenly under the presser foot.

Fuse interfacing to leather.

2. Use heavyweight thread, such as topstitching or upholstery thread, and choose a longer stitch length to avoid perforating the leather and tearing it. Don't backstitch at the beginning or end of a seam; instead, tie off thread tails on the wrong side of the leather. When topstitching, use a longer stitch length.

Use heavy thread and a longer stitch.

3. Don't use pins. Double-sided tape or specialty leather tape (available at macpheeworkshop.com) holds leather without slipping, and makes necessary repositioning of hems or seam allowances easy. Lightweight fabric glues suitable for leather will bond more permanently and won't allow for easy adjustments. Use glue only when

you're comfortable and sure you won't need to pull pieces apart.

Secure leather with tape.

4. Use binder clips instead of pattern weights or pins to secure pattern pieces to the leather while cutting.

5. *Do not* iron leather. Finger-press all seam allowances open. Seam allowances will still gravitate back toward each other, but repeated manipulation will help. Apply a small amount of glue between the seam allowance and fabric wrong side using a cotton swab if desired, or topstitch the seam allowances in place for a functional but decorative detail.

Finger-press seam allowances open.

6. In thick areas, such as bulky seam allowances or hems, pound the leather slightly using a mallet or hammer to make the leather more pliable and flat. Turn the machine wheel by hand when sewing very thick layers. Some leather is too thick for home sewing machines to handle—stick with lightweight cow, lamb, and pigskin.

7. Use a new size 100/16 leather needle for each project. The punching needle tip creates a clean hole with every stitch. (Do not use a leather needle on other fabrics.)

8. A Teflon presser foot and throat plate help leather slide through the machine and reduce possible damage to the leather surface. A regular foot and throat plate may be used; however, apply the lightest pressure setting available for the presser foot to avoid crushing or distorting the hide. Adjusting the presser foot pressure can be tricky depending on the machine. Mark the current setting using tape or a grease pen so you'll be able to set the machine back to "normal" once leather sewing is complete. Consult the machine manual and stitch first on leather scraps to ensure the perfect setting.

9. Leave leather edges raw—there's no need to serge- or zigzag-finish the edges because leather doesn't ravel.

Leave leather edges raw.

10. Go slowly! Until you're completely comfortable with sewing leather, stitch slowly and carefully.

# SEWING WITH MICROFIBER FLEECE

As you become more experienced and sew on different types of fabrics, you'll quickly learn that each fabric has its own personality. Some are more agreeable than others. Even if you're a beginner, you don't have to limit yourself to fabrics that are considered easy to sew. Luxuriously soft and cuddly microfiber fleeces like Minky and Cuddle Up are wonderful for making robes, backing baby quilts, and more. These super-soft fabrics are a cinch to sew with these nine helpful tips.

1.  Microfiber fleece is a polyester fabric. Because it doesn't shrink, you don't have to prewash. If you're using a natural-fiber fabric, such as cotton, in the same project as the microfiber fleece, prewash the natural-fiber fabric to avoid distortion when the finished project is laundered.

2.  Microfiber fleeces have nap. When cutting out the pattern, place all pattern pieces with the nap running down the garment. To determine the nap, run your hand along the fabric length—it feels smooth when stroked with the nap. Because light hits upward- and downward-facing naps differently, the same fabric can appear as two distinct shades if garment pieces are cut in different directions.

3.  Microfiber fleece doesn't ravel, and sewing it is very similar to sewing other fleece.

4.  Microfiber fleece is prone to shedding at cut edges. Zigzag, pink, or serge the seams to finish them and minimize shedding. An adhesive lint roller is helpful for picking up loose fibers.

5.  The fabric's lengthwise grain (parallel to the selvage) has very little stretch, while the crosswise grain stretches noticeably. Pay attention to grainline placement when cutting out patterns. After cutting, grasp the fabric edge and pull off the loose fibers to minimize shedding as you work. An adhesive lint roller or even a mini vacuum cleaner can be a great help in keeping the shedding under control.

6.  Use a size 80/12 universal sewing-machine needle. Microfiber fleece produces a lot of lint, so clean the fibers from the bobbin case and feed dogs regularly while sewing.

7.  Microfiber fleece tends to be slippery. When sewing layers together, place pins close together to keep the edges from curling and to minimize fabric creeping. Use the machine's feed dogs to help control fullness and stretch: when joining a stable lengthwise edge to a stretchy crosswise edge, place the stretchy edge on the bottom as it feeds through the machine; when joining microfiber fleece to woven fabric, place the fleece underneath the woven fabric.

8.  Press microfiber fleece with care. Too much heat or heavy steaming will relax the fabric, removing heat-set details such as dimensional dots. Adjust the iron to its synthetic setting and don't use steam. Press lightly on the wrong side in the direction of the nap to avoid crushing it. Press seam allowances open to reduce bulk. If you must press from the right side, use a press cloth. Using only the iron tip, press along the well of the seam. When pressing textured microfiber fleece, be especially careful to avoid flattening the design.

9.  To raise nap caught in the stitching or pressed in the wrong direction, brush the fabric with a small, clean soft brush.

# SEWING WITH NYLON

Nylon's not just for tents—it's available in myriad colors and textures, so it's perfect for all sorts of sewing projects from compact reusable shopping bags to rugged covers for stadium seat cushions. Nylon is a strong, durable, machine-washable, quick-drying synthetic fiber. It's often blended with other fibers to increase resistance to wear, reduce wrinkles, and enhance washing and drying characteristics.

Nylon comes in many different forms, generic and trademarked, including taffeta, Supplex, oxford, ripstop, packcloth, Cordura, and ballistic. With so many names and surface treatments, it can be hard to decide which one to use for your project. One way to distinguish among nylon types is to check the denier number. Denier is a unit of weight that correlates to the diameter of the nylon yarns. A smaller denier number means finer thread, such as a 70 denier taffeta, while a larger denier is coarser, such as 1000 denier ballistic nylon or Cordura.

## SUPPLIES

**Thread.** Choose long-staple 100% polyester thread for extra strength. Using high-quality polyester thread instead of all-purpose thread will reduce the occurrence of skipped stitches.

**Needles.** Sewing-machine-needle types are defined by their points. A universal needle has a tapered modified ball point that makes it appropriate for sewing on most fabric types. Sharp-point needles are designed with fine shafts to pierce densely woven fabrics as well as fabrics with water-repellent finishes. A jeans needle has a sharp point that makes it ideal for sewing on tough fabrics and tightly-woven twills, such as denim. A Microtex needle is a very fine, especially sharp needle that's designed for synthetic fabrics, such as nylon and polyester.

Choose the needle that's most compatible with the weight of your nylon fabric. For lightweight nylon, such as taffeta, use a needle size 60/8; for 200 denier oxford nylon, choose size 70/10; for mediumweight nylon, such as 420 denier packcloth, use size 80/12; for heavyweight nylon, such as 500 to 600 denier Cordura, use size 90/14; and for fabrics such as 1000-denier ballistic nylon, choose 100/16. Nylon fabric will wear down the needle point, so you may need to change the needle frequently.

**Pins.** Pins and needles leave permanent holes in nylon fabric. To prevent unwanted holes, pin only within the seam allowance, or keep the fabric layers together with large paperclips, binder clips, or tape. Slide the paperclips onto the fabric edge only part way so that they're easy to slide off and to avoid snagging the fabric with the sharp paperclip point.

## TAKE CARE

Before cutting out your pattern pieces, remove any wrinkles in the nylon fabric. Begin pressing with a warm iron and gradually increase the iron heat until the fabric is flattened enough. Proceed with caution; a high temperature may melt the nylon fibers. To protect the iron plate, use a press cloth or two layers of tissue paper. If you come across a very stubborn pleat or crease, increase the iron temperature slightly and use a damp press cloth to cover the fabric. Nylon is thermoplastic, meaning heat-set creases are permanent; removing a crease requires a higher temperature setting than that used to make the crease, but not high enough to melt the fibers. Always test by pressing on a scrap first.

Most nylon fabrics are suitable for machine washing and tumble drying on low heat; however, coated nylon fabric may need special care. After cutting out the fabric, save scraps to use for test samples. Cut a 6" nylon square and toss it in the washer and dryer. Then check the test sample for fraying, wrinkling, and coating quality. Sprinkle water on the washed test sample and on an unwashed fabric to check for any difference in water repellency.

## NO FRAY

Uncoated nylon fabric edges tend to fray and ravel and will continue to do so if left untreated. To prevent fraying, seal the raw edges by searing, binding, or applying liquid seam sealant. Test any method first on a fabric scrap.

**Searing.** Light a candle in a well-ventilated room. Hold the fabric edge taut near the base of the flame. Quickly move the fabric edge along next to the flame, carefully keeping the body of the fabric away from the flame. If a large brown bead forms, move the fabric farther away from the flame or move it more quickly. The objective is to melt the edge fibers just enough to stop any fraying that might occur.

**Binding.** Binding prevents the fabric edge from fraying and provides abrasion resistance. Use prefolded bias tape or twill tape to cover the seam allowances. After sewing the seam, sandwich the seam allowances in the tape fold and clip or pin; zigzag-stitch the tape in place. The seam allowances can be bound together or individually.

**Seam Sealant.** Various types and brands of seam sealant are available at fabric stores or online. Check the fabric-care instructions on the bottle label to make sure the sealant is compatible with the intended use of your nylon project. Follow the manufacturer's instructions to apply the sealant. Test on a fabric scrap to learn whether the sealant will change the fabric color; if it does, confine the sealant to seam allowance edges that will be hidden inside the project and take extra care not to leave stray drops on the body of the fabric.

## SMOOTH SEWING

Nylon collects static electricity. As you sew, nylon fabric tends to cling to the sewing-machine needle, sometimes resulting in puckered stitches. Test by sewing on a nylon scrap and try these tips to prevent puckering.

- Hold the fabric firmly as you sew, with one hand in front of the machine and one hand in back.
- Change the sewing-machine throat plate to a straight-stitch plate, which has a single circular hole rather than the wide slot for zigzag stitching.
- Use a straight-stitch sewing-machine presser foot.
- Fill the bobbin on a very low speed to prevent the thread from stretching.

Oh So Durable
A nylon filament thread is stronger than a steel wire of the same weight.

What to Make?
Here are some fun project ideas to try out your nylon know-how.

- Drawstring gym sack or laundry bag
- Reusable grocery bag
- Running shorts
- iPod armband
- Cell-phone pouch
- Kite
- Windsock
- Lunch bag
- Apron
- Banner or flag
- Wallet
- Windbreaker

# SEWING WITH OILCLOTH

Oilcloth is a unique textile that's not only sturdy and waterproof, but also adds a fun retro twist to your sewing projects. Historically, it was made by applying layers of linseed oil (hence the name) to one side of a sturdy canvas or duck fabric. You can still occasionally find examples of this cloth, but nowadays most oilcloth is manufactured with a more-durable, less-sticky vinyl coating instead. One thing that's remained the same is the wide variety of cheerful, colorful prints in which oilcloth is available, making it the ideal fabric to brighten up your kitchen or patio. Here are some pointers for working with it.

## FLATTEN IT OUT

Before you begin to sew oilcloth, remove any folds or creases. Spread out the fabric in a warm spot, such as under a sunny window, for a little while. The creases should disappear on their own. For even faster results, lay the oilcloth flat and use a hairdryer for a few minutes to warm and relax the creases, or briefly iron the wrong side of the fabric using very low heat.

## PINS AND NEEDLES

When sewing multiple oilcloth layers together, avoid using pins, as they leave permanent, unsightly holes. Instead, secure the layers with masking tape, binder clips, or paper clips. Use a size 90/14 or 100/16 jeans/denim or Sharp needle that can handle stiffer materials like the canvas often used in oilcloth.

## SEW AHEAD

Take it slow. You can't just rip out a seam on oilcloth if you make a mistake, since the needle leaves little holes behind. Before you begin a project, test sew on an oilcloth scrap to see what, if any, adjustments you need to make to your machine settings.

Set the machine to a slightly longer stitch length. If your stitches are too short, the needle will perforate the fabric too many times, which can result in tearing. Use a 3 to 4 mm stitch length for straight seams. Shorten the stitches around curves and sew slowly for more control.

It's generally easier to sew on the oilcloth wrong side because its texture is similar to regular canvas fabric. If you want to stitch on the right side, such as for topstitching, use a Teflon foot or roller foot to prevent sticking. Place a layer of tear-away stabilizer, masking tape, or tissue paper over the oilcloth to avoid having the machine foot touch the sticky surface. Be sure the stabilizer or tape is easy to remove completely after sewing.

Oilcloth doesn't ravel, so it's not imperative to finish the edges. Leave them raw, trim them with pinking shears, apply bias or twill tape, or sew a single-turn hem.

### Oilcloth Originals

Oilcloth is strong, stain resistant, and waterproof, so it lends itself fabulously to many projects you might not be able to make with regular fabric. Here are just a few ideas.

- Any type of apron for cooking, crafts, cleaning, gardening, or other hobbies
- Lunch bag
- Baby bib
- Outdoor chair cushions
- Tablecloth, table runner, or place mats
- Book cover
- Pencil or cosmetic pouch
- Shopping or beach tote
- Sewing-machine cover
- Shelf or drawer liner

# BUILD YOUR EMBELLISHING SKILLS

# HAND EMBROIDERY

Hand embroidery has made a comeback, and stitchers have brought the designs from medieval to modern. The fresh take on this ancient art form is appearing on everything from jeans and sweaters to accessories and home decor, and the best part is that you can make the stitches any length or style to suit your design.

Basic hand embroidery is proof that you don't need a top-of-the-line sewing machine to create beautifully embellished projects. Armed with these simple stitches, you can embellish a denim skirt or turn a home or fashion accessory into a showpiece. Any piece of fabric or textile item becomes a potential canvas for the color, texture, and style of embroidery with just a simple needle and thread.

Embroidery floss is made up of six thread strands and is sold by the skein. Remove the paper band holding the skein together and unwind an 18" length. Separate the strands needed by slowly pulling the strands apart at one end, letting the remainder untwist as you pull.

### Handy Hint
The following instructions are for right-handed sewing. If you're left-handed, reverse them. It may also be helpful to view the drawings in a mirror.

### Fiber Is Important
Wool thread will shrink when washed and dried; some cotton threads may shrink and bleed. Use a synthetic thread, cotton floss, or pearl cotton labeled *colorfast* when stitching on a garment or accessory that will be cleaned.

## RUNNING STITCH

Knot the long end of the thread. Bring the thread up from the wrong side at 1. Insert the needle at 2, up at 3, down at 4, and up at 5. Pull the thread through. Keep the stitches about twice as long as the spaces between them for the stitch as shown; experiment with different stitch lengths and spaces for more variety. Knot the thread on the wrong side at the end of the last stitch.

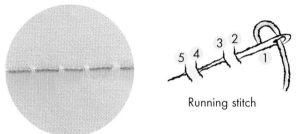

Running stitch

## BACKSTITCH

Knot the thread. Bring the needle up through the fabric at 1, down at 2, back up at 3, and down again at 1. Repeat as necessary, following the traced line. Knot the thread on the wrong side at the end of the last stitch.

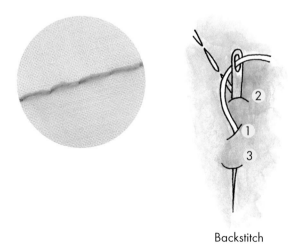

Backstitch

## CHAIN STITCH

Knot the thread. Bring the thread up from the wrong side at 1. Make a loop to the left, holding the loop with your left thumb. Insert the needle at 2 (very close to 1) and bring it up at 3, emerging within the thread loop. Pull the needle and thread through the loop, but not too tightly. Repeat by inserting the needle inside the first loop at 4 and back up at 5. Continue until the entire design line is covered. End by inserting the needle outside the loop of the last stitch; knot the thread on the wrong side.

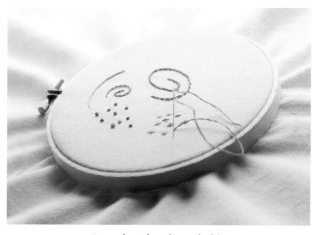

An embroidery hoop holds
the fabric taut to eliminate puckers.

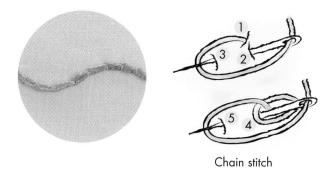

Chain stitch

## CROSS-STITCH

Bring the needle up through the fabric at 1 and down at 2; pull the stitch to lie flat against the fabric. Come up at 3 and down at 4; pull the thread taut. When making a series of cross-stitches, be sure the top stitch lies in the same direction in each stitch.

Cross-stitch

## LAZY DAISY

This is a variation of chain stitch; essentially, each lazy daisy is a single link of the chain. Bring the needle up through the fabric at 1, down at 2 and up at 3, emerging within the thread loop. Pull the needle and thread through the fabric, leaving enough slack to produce a pleasing loop of thread. Take the needle down at 4, making a tiny stitch over the previous thread to anchor the loop.

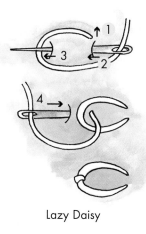

Lazy Daisy

## SEED STITCH

Knot the thread. Take small stitches in random directions to create an irregular pattern of short stitches. Knot the thread on the wrong side at the end of the last stitch.

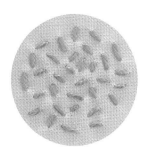

Seed stitch

## SATIN STITCH

A satin stitch is used to completely fill an area with stitches that are made close beside each other. Knot the thread. Bring the thread up at 1, down at 2, and up at 3, which is directly beside 1. Bring the needle down at 4 and up at 5. Keep the stitches within the shape being filled; position them closely enough to cover the shape completely without piling up. Knot the thread on the fabric wrong side at the end of the last stitch.

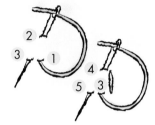

Satin stitch

## FRENCH KNOT

Bring the needle up through the fabric at 1. Holding the thread with your other hand, wrap it around the needle two or three times. Pinching the wraps lightly with the hand holding the needle to keep the thread taut, insert the needle down at 2, right next to 1. Pull the needle and floss through to the back of the fabric, maintaining tension on the thread with your left hand until the knot rests on the fabric surface.

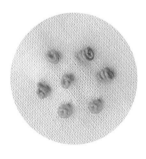

French knot

# COUCHING

Couching is an easy embellishment that adds texture and dimension to projects. To couch, lay a length of yarn or other fiber (such as string, hemp, or embroidery thread) over the fabric and attach it to the surface with machine or hand stitches worked with a finer thread. The fiber is referred to as the "laid" thread because it's positioned, or laid, over the fabric surface.

Select a decorative fiber that matches or contrasts with the fabric. Decide whether to couch the fiber by hand or machine. Select a thread in a matching or contrasting color, depending on the finished appearance you desire. If you're stitching by hand, colorful embroidery floss offers myriad design possibilities. If you're stitching by machine, variegated thread is a fun option. Couching with invisible thread is also a great choice for either sewing method—it's very forgiving (you can fudge a straight line and no one will know) and allows you to see the entire laid fiber after it's stitched.

## COUCHING BY MACHINE

Yellow yarn couched by
machine with dark thread

1. Measure the laid-thread width. Set the machine for a zigzag about 3 mm long that's a bit wider than the laid thread; the stitches should fall close to the laid-fiber edges without puncturing the fiber. Test stitch a sample to ensure the stitch-length setting leaves plenty of the laid fiber visible.

2. For smooth, pucker-free couching, stabilize the fabric wrong side using appropriate stabilizer for the fabric. For corduroy fabric, heavyweight tear-away stabilizer is a good choice; for lightweight batiste, an adhesive, water-soluble stabilizer might be used. Search the Internet or go to www.sewnews.com to find the best stabilizer for the chosen fabric. Test the stabilizer to make sure it works with the fabric before stitching on the actual project, and consider ease of removability as well.

### Pucker Up

Omitting stabilizer causes the fabric to pucker between the couched lines, which could be a very cool design element.

3. Plan a design and use a fabric marker to draw the design on the fabric right side. Position the yarn on the drawn lines; pin by using straight pins to trap the laid fiber against the fabric. Stitch over the yarn with a zigzag stitch. You may want to try free-form couching instead: place a fiber

strand over the fabric, hand-guide it into position, and then stitch over it—no marking or pinning required.

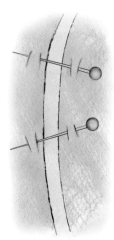

Use pins to trap the fiber
against the background fabric.

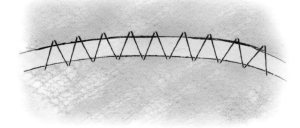

Zigzag stitch over a
laid fiber to couch it.

4. Remove the stabilizer following the manufacturer's instructions.

## COUCHING BY HAND

1. Draw a design on the fabric right side using a fabric-marking pen. If you're free-form couching, skip this step.

2. Stabilize the wrong side of the couching area. If the design is intricate, or you require a more stable work surface, hoop the fabric. Use an embroidery hoop that's bigger than the chosen design and center the design within the hoop. Pin the fiber over the drawn lines. For free-form couching, pin one fiber end in place to begin.

3. Knot the thread and bring it up through the fabric alongside the fiber end. Take a stitch over the fiber and back down through the fabric on the opposite side to hold the fiber in place. Continue stitching,

either removing pins as you couch or holding down the fiber as you go.

Couching a fiber by hand

4. At the end of the design, secure the fiber end with one last stitch and bring the thread to the fabric wrong side. Leave a long thread tail and weave it through the stitches on the wrong side. Carefully remove the stabilizer following the manufacturer's instructions.

When couching by hand,
space the stitches to reveal the laid fiber.

### Even or Odd
Vary the spacing between stitches for a funky, random look.

## KNOW BEFORE YOU SEW

Cut a few lengths of the fiber(s) you plan to use and place them on the fabric. Consider these questions:

- Do the fiber colors work with the fabric and with each other? If the design isn't balanced or pleasing to the eye, remove one or all of the fibers, or try a different fabric.

- Is the fiber flexible enough to maneuver around design curves? If not, modify the design to better suit the fiber's flexibility, or choose a different fiber to couch.

- Will a zigzag stitch lend itself to a fun design? Experiment with decorative stitches, such as the blind hem or feather stitch, to achieve additional decorative elements.

- Is the standard tension setting on the machine appropriate to accommodate the fiber? If not, loosen the upper tension so the machine can handle the bulk. Always practice on a test scrap before couching on the project fabric.

## NEAT FEET

There are six different presser feet well suited for couching by machine. If the laid thread isn't bulky, a regular presser foot may work fine. If a regular presser foot doesn't work, try one of these specialty feet; always test the feet and stitches with scraps to ensure the desired look on the project.

**A multi-cord foot** handles several fibers at once. Multiple holes on the foot allow you to feed five to seven different fibers through at once, creating multicolored design details.

Multi-cord foot

**A beading foot** deftly applies bead strands or a string of rhinestones to fabric. The foot has a notched underside that accommodates both the width and height of bead strands for easy, guided placement.

Beading foot

**An open-toe embroidery foot** accommodates all types of couching materials. Its design allows for an unobstructed view of the strands as they're guided and couched. The free-motion model on the left works for free-form couching with the feed dogs lowered.

Open-toe embroidery feet

**A braiding foot** has a groove on the underside that accommodates thicker yarn, braid, trims, cords, and piping. It has an opening in front through which the couching fiber passes.

Braiding foot

**A cording/couching foot** allows you to feed small fibers such as yarn or ribbon through a small loop attached to the foot. Place the fabric under the foot, feed the fiber through the loop from top to bottom, and guide it to the needle. Take a stitch to catch the fiber; then continue sewing with the chosen couching stitch.

Cording/couching foot

# FUSIBLE APPLIQUÉ

Spice up any project by adding appliqué. It's a quick and easy way to transform a project from dull to dazzling.

1. When working with fusible web, shapes must be traced in reverse to appear correctly oriented in the finished design. Trace each appliqué shape in reverse on the paper side of the fusible web.

2. Roughly cut out the appliqué shapes slightly outside the drawn lines.

3. Fuse the web to the appliqué fabric wrong side, following the manufacturer's instructions.

Fuse the roughly cut shapes to the appliqué fabric wrong side.

# YO-YOS

4. Cut out the appliqué shapes on the drawn lines; remove the paper.

5. Working on an ironing board, position the appliqués on the project right side to create the design. Place the fusible side of each appliqué against the right side of the project. Cover with a press cloth; press to fuse in place.

6. Set up the sewing machine for a satin zigzag stitch (0.3 to 0.5 mm long, 2 to 3 mm wide). Thread the machine with matching or contrasting thread, depending on the desired effect. Test the stitch on scrap fabric to ensure the stitch covers the fabric edge completely without gaps or bunching.

7. Satin stitch around the outer edges of the appliqué. Position the stitch so one swing of the needle falls just beside the appliqué fabric, entering the background fabric only, while the other needle swing falls in the appliqué itself.

Use a satin zigzag stitch to secure the appliqués to the project.

Making yo-yos is a great way to use fabric scraps left over from other projects. Originally yo-yos were pieced together to make quilts or appliqués, but these fabric medallions are now used for all sorts of embellishments. Make yo-yos in different sizes and experiment with layering them or adding buttons and beads for extra dimension. Picture their potential uses (a funky pin, jean or jacket trim, a cover for an old purse, a belt, curtains, etc.). This is a small project that's done by hand, so you can take fabric circles with you and stitch up a yo-yo virtually anywhere.

## INSTRUCTIONS

1. Items you'll need: scrap fabric (twice as large as the finished yo-yo), hand-sewing needle, matching all-purpose thread, compass or round object (twice the finished yo-yo diameter), and a fabric-marking pen or pencil.

2. Determine the size of the finished yo-yo. Multiply that number by two to determine the diameter of the fabric circle. For example, to make a 3"-wide yo-yo, cut a 6"-diameter circle.

3. Use a compass and pencil to draw a circle of the determined size on the fabric wrong side. If you'll be making many yo-yos, create a template of cardboard or plastic rather than drawing each circle individually with a compass. To make yo-yos without a compass, use a fabric-marking pen to trace a circular object that's the correct size, such as a CD, plate, or plastic lid.

4. Cut the fabric ¼" outside the drawn circle. Thread a needle with one strand of thread that's long enough to stitch around the entire circle plus 4". Knot the thread end a few times so the knot won't pop through the fabric.

Cut the fabric ¼" outside the drawn circle.

5. Fold about ½" of the circle raw edge to the wrong side along the drawn line. Hold the fabric fold in your fingers with the wrong side facing you. Insert the needle from the right side and bring it through the folded fabric to the wrong side. Stitch around the circle with ¼"-long running stitches, folding more seam allowance to the wrong side as needed. When you reach the original starting point, end with the needle on the fabric right side.

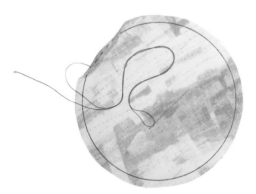

Fold the edge to the wrong side and sew a running stitch around the circle, near the fold.

6. Carefully pull the thread to gather the fabric. Work the gathers around the circle to the beginning stitch. Keep gathering until the stitched circle edge is drawn completely together (for larger yo-yos,

there may be a small gap because the gathers are too thick to pull all the way to the center).

Work the gathers around the circle to the starting point of the stitching.

7. Take a few stitches in one of the yo-yo gathers to secure the thread. Tie a knot and trim the thread close to the knot. Center the gathers on the yo-yo. You should have enough thread on the needle to stitch another yo-yo.

Center the gathers on the yo-yo.

8. To stitch yo-yos together, position two yo-yos with their gathered sides facing each other. With a needle and knotted thread, make a few small whipstitches through the yo-yos at the outer folds. Secure the thread with a knot; clip the thread close to the knot. Use coordinating thread and hide the thread tails between yo-yo layers for a less-visible join.

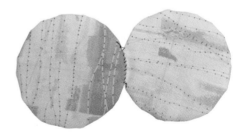

Whipstitch yo-yos together for larger projects.

# QUILTING

Yo-yos in different sizes and colors add interest to projects.

Quilting is the process of stitching together three fabric layers: the quilt top, the batting, and the backing fabric (often called the quilt sandwich). It's not the same as patchwork or piecing, which are typically completed before quilting begins. When the quilting is done, bind the edges to finish the job; see "Double-Fold Binding" on page 57 for more information. Quilting may seem intimidating, but it's really not—just take it one step at a time.

## MARKING

1. Trace the quilting motif onto tracing paper. Place the tracing paper under the quilt top with a light source behind to mark the quilt top. As an alternative, use a stencil placed on top of the quilt to mark the design for stitching. Lightly mark the design on the quilt top with a hard lead pencil or a marker of your choice. Always test the marking product for removability before using it on your quilt top.

2. Straight lines may be "marked" as you quilt by using masking tape that's pulled away after quilting along its edge. Your machine accessories may include a quilting gauge that attaches to the presser foot to aid in stitching parallel lines with no marking at all.

## BACKING AND PREPARATION

1. Make the quilt backing 4" to 8" larger than the quilt top (2" to 4" on each side). Usually two or three fabric lengths must be sewn together; remove the fabric selvages before stitching to avoid puckers. Press the seam allowances open.

2. Place the backing wrong side up on a flat surface. Smooth the backing to remove all wrinkles and tape or pin the fabric edges to the surface, keeping the backing taut but not stretched out of shape or off grain.

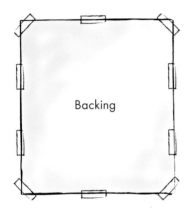

Tape the backing to keep it taut.

3. Smooth the batting over the backing.

4. Center the quilt top right side up over the batting.

5. Pin the layers as necessary to secure them while basting.

## BASTING

The most traditional method for basting quilts is by hand, with needle and thread. Beginning in the center of the quilt, hand-baste horizontal and vertical lines 4" to 6" apart.

Hand basting is the traditional way to stabilize layers for quilting.

Many modern quilters prefer to baste with rustproof safety pins; it's the preferred method for basting quilts that will be machine quilted, and it stabilizes the quilt layers better than hand-basting stitches. Begin at the center and place pins 3" to 4" apart across the entire quilt, avoiding lines to be quilted.

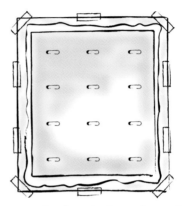

Basting with safety pins is another option.

Quilts can also be basted with a temporary aerosol basting spray. To use, spray the backing fabric wrong side before smoothing the batting into place and spray the batting before adding the quilt top to the quilt sandwich.

## THE QUILTING STITCHES

You have the choice to quilt by hand or machine. Here are two common quilting terms that can apply to either quilting method:

*Quilting in the ditch* refers to stitching on top of the existing seam, or, in hand quilting, right next to the seamline on the side without seam allowances.

*Outline quilting* refers to quilting ¼" from the seamline or from the perimeter of an appliquéd shape.

## HAND QUILTING

Hand quilting is a short running stitch, sewn with a single strand of thread that pierces all three layers of the quilt sandwich.

1. Use a short needle (8 or 9 between) with about 18" of thread. Make a small knot in the thread end.

2. Take a long first stitch (about 1") through the top and batting only, coming up where the quilting will begin. Tug on the thread to pull the knotted end between the layers.

3. Take short even stitches that are the same size on the top and back of the quilt. Push the needle with a thimble on the middle finger of your dominant hand; guide the fabric in front of the needle with the thumb of the working hand above the quilt and with the middle finger of the other hand under the quilt.

Take short, even stitches using both hands to guide the needle.

4. To end a line of quilting, make a small knot in the thread close to the quilt top, push the needle through the top and batting only, and bring it to the surface about 1" away; tug the thread until the knot pops through the quilt top, burying the knot in the batting. Clip the thread close to the quilt surface.

Focus on Quilting
Use contrasting thread to make the quilting designs pop.

## MACHINE QUILTING

In general, there are two types of machine quilting: machine-guided and free-motion quilting.

Machine-guided quilting is most practical for straight-line designs or those that require minimal pivoting and direction changes. A walking foot is often used for straight-line or in-the-ditch quilting.

Free-motion quilting gives the operator full control of the machine's stitching speed and direction. The quilt can be moved sideways, on the diagonal, or along a curved path in addition to the forward and backward motions of machine-guided work. To free-motion quilt, drop or cover the feed dogs and use a darning foot.

Before quilting, bring the bobbin thread to the top of the quilt so it doesn't get caught as you sew. Lower the presser foot, hold the needle thread, and move the needle through one down-and-up cycle. Lift the presser foot to release the thread tension, and gently tug on the needle thread to draw a loop of the bobbin thread to the top of the quilt. Pull the bobbin thread end to the top. Lower the needle into the same hole created by the initial stitch, lower the presser foot, and begin quilting.

Starting and Stopping
Rather than backstitching, begin and end each line of quilting with ¼" of very short stitches to secure the thread.

1. Prepare the quilt sandwich as described in "Backing and Preparation" and "Basting" on page 89.

2. Thread the machine as desired for the project. Set the stitch length for 3 mm. To quilt straight lines or gentle curves, you may want to use the machine's walking foot or even-feed attachment.

3. Begin stitching in the center of the project and work your way toward the edges. The layers tend to shift as you sew, even when basted. Beginning at the center allows any extra fullness in the layers to be dispersed at the edges, reducing the chance of creating tucks in the fabric. Remove basting pins as you come to them.

4. Quilt your project using one of the following methods:
   - *Stitch in the ditch*, following the seamlines and stitching with the needle in the well of the seam. Secure the threads at the beginning and end of each line of stitching.

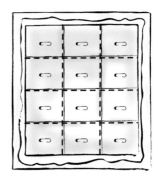

Stitching in the ditch is a simple way to quilt.

- *Channel quilting*, stitching parallel rows of straight lines going in one direction across the project. Mark the lines on your project using chalk, an air-soluble marking pen, or lengths of masking tape. You can use a quilting gauge that attaches to the presser foot to guide parallel lines, or eyeball the distance between the rows for a more irregular effect.

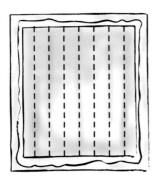

Channel quilting makes use of parallel lines.

- *Grid quilting*, stitching parallel rows of straight lines in one direction across the project, and then following with straight lines in the perpendicular direction to form a grid.

Grid quilting uses parallel lines in two different directions.

## PREPARING FOR BINDING

1. Baste around the quilt ³⁄₁₆" from the quilt-top edges. Trim the batting and backing to match the quilt top.

2. To add a sleeve to the quilt for hanging, see "Sleeve for Hanging" below.

3. To prepare the binding strips and bind the quilt, refer to "Double-Fold Binding" on page 57.

## SLEEVE FOR HANGING

The long upper sleeve edge can be caught in the seam when the binding is sewn to the quilt, so prepare the hanging sleeve before the binding. Be sure the sleeve ends are not caught in the binding seams.

1. Plan to make the sleeve 2" to 4" shorter than the quilt width. Cut strips 6" wide across the fabric width (or as directed in the pattern) and join them to create the length needed. Press the seam allowances to one side.

2. Hem the sleeve short ends by pressing ½" to the wrong side, and then folding and pressing once more; topstitch close to the hem edge.

3. Fold the sleeve in half lengthwise with wrong sides together; match the raw edges.

4. Center the sleeve along the top edge of the quilt back, matching the raw edges; baste.

5. Sew the binding to the quilt.

6. Once the binding is sewn, smooth the sleeve against the backing and blindstitch along the sleeve lower edge and along the underlayer of each end, catching some of the batting in the stitches.

Blindstitch the sleeve edges to the quilt back.

# NEEDLE FELTING

Needle felting is the process of using barbed needles to force fiber layers together, entangling the individual fibers for a permanent bond. There are different types of felting, accomplished with and without needles, such as flat-surface design, dimensional designs, wet felting, and dry felting. In this section we'll discuss dry, flat-surface needle felting. Flat-surface work is done directly on the right side of the fabric or piece that's being felted.

## NEEDLES

The most important tool for needle felting is the needle. A felting needle is very sharp and has tiny barbs. You can use a single needle or a multi-needle tool, which has several needles attached to a handle. A multi-needle tool lets you cover more area at a faster rate. The handle also makes the needles easier to hold and work with.

### Safety First

Felting needles are very sharp, and the barbs make them even more dangerous. Keep your fingers away from the stabbing needles while felting. Always store needles in a protective sleeve when not in use, and keep them away from children.

## PROTECTIVE BASE

Since needle felting involves punching sharp needles up and down repeatedly, you need something to protect your work surface from damage.

Foam is a common protective choice. The size of the foam block can vary depending on project size, but make sure the foam is very dense. Replace the foam when it begins to deteriorate from repeated punching.

Another option is a brush mat, which is like an inverted scrub brush. The felting needle should be shorter than the bristles, so it can enter the brush safely without hitting its backing, which can easily break the needle.

## FIBERS

Many different types of fabric work as the base fabric—just make sure that the needles can easily pass through, and be aware of how the felting needles will affect the base fabric's durability and integrity. Good fabric choices include all types of wool, some knits, sweaters, denim (not stretch denim), lightweight fabrics, fleece, burlap, and upholstery fabric. It's always a good idea to test the fabric before beginning a project.

There are also several choices for the fiber to be felted into the base material. Wool is the first choice for felting because its structure is perfect for melding with other fibers. Wool is available as fabric, yarn, and roving. Other fabrics and fibers that work, producing very different effects, include silk, mohair, organdy, organza, and netting. Again, always test before diving into the actual project.

## DESIGNS

There are lots of options for needle-felting designs. Draw a design freehand, trace around a cookie cutter, use a design supplied by a pattern or book, or use a stencil. Start with simple shapes and a minimum of detailing while you're learning to needle felt.

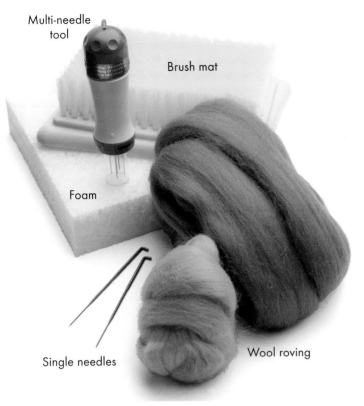

Multi-needle tool

Brush mat

Foam

Single needles

Wool roving

## NEEDLE FELTING BY HAND

1. Draw the design on the base fabric. Use a removable marker or plan to cover the outline completely with felted fibers.

2. Position yarn, fiber, or fabric over the drawn design.

Lay the fiber on the base fabric freehand or follow a sketched design.

3. Take a few stabs into the fiber to baste it in place. Stab straight up and down; angling and twisting are more likely to break the needle. Stab only deep enough for the barbs to pass through the fabric. Stabbing too deeply forces fiber into the work surface (i.e., the foam or brush mat).

4. Don't move the fibers with the needle—the needle might break. Use a pair of tweezers or a double-pointed needle to move fibers.

5. After basting the design and checking its placement, repeatedly punch the fibers into the fabric base using a straight up-and-down motion. Hold the needle or multi-needle tool firmly. Push down and pull up in a repetitive motion using a consistent speed to cover the area you're felting. Continue until the fiber is secured to the base layer.

Use an up-and-down motion to punch fibers into the base fabric.

## NEEDLE FELTING BY MACHINE

A needle-felting machine is a pricier option than hand-held needles. There are machines designed just for felting, and there are sewing machines that have attachments/adapter kits for felting.

Felting on a machine is similar to free-motion quilting—the machine doesn't feed the fabric through as it does in regular sewing. You control the motion of the fabric. There's no thread in the machine, just multiple needles that punch the fabric at high speed.

You can spend anywhere from a few hundred dollars to more than $1,000 for a needle-felting machine. For more information, check out the following websites to see what these companies offer:

- www.babylock.com
- www.berninausa.com
- www.brothersews.com
- www.feltcrafts.com
- www.husqvarnaviking.com
- www.janome.com
- www.nancysnotions.com
- www.pfaffusa.com

# FABRIC FOILING

Bring fabric projects to life with instant glitz and shine. Foiling directly onto fabric is easy, fun, and permanent. This chapter details several techniques for applying foil, but if the foil or adhesive you're using has specific manufacturer's instructions, follow them exactly. In any case, always test the method first to ensure the desired results.

## TOOLS OF THE TRADE

Wooden craft stick

Press cloth

Adhesive

Foil sheets

Freezer paper

**Foil.** Foil is usually packaged in sheets and is available in a number of dazzling colors. Each foil sheet is shiny on one side and slightly dull on the other. The dull side is the actual foil and the shiny side is the plastic covering that will be peeled away during the foiling process.

**Fabric.** Your fabric must be clean and perfectly flat. Prewash and press the fabric before beginning.

**Adhesive.** This is what makes the foil stick to the fabric. There are several options to choose from; see "Adhesives" below.

**Freezer paper.** This household item adds stability when fused to fabric. It's also used to create stencils.

**Press cloth.** A press cloth is required for the heat method. It protects the foil from coming in direct contact with the iron, which will damage both.

**Bone folder, wooden craft stick, or paperclip.** Any of these items can be used for the burnishing method. Stroke the foil with any of these tools to transfer the foil to the fabric.

## ADHESIVES

The foil is as permanent as the adhesive you choose. In general, less glue is best.

1. Apply the glue with a toothbrush, sea sponge, fingertip, or a stamp.

2. Let the glue dry before applying the foil. Some glues will be tacky when dry; follow package instructions for the length of waiting time before the glue is ready to foil.

3. Choose one of the following adhesives. When in doubt, test different types to find the one that works best and fits your comfort zone.

   - *Liquid adhesive* lets you draw designs directly onto the fabric.

   - *Flexible glue* works well on stretchy fabric.

   - *Double-sided tape* can be used only if you're working on material that will never be washed.

   - *Paper-backed fusible web* can also be used to create stencils. Cut the shapes from the web, place the web adhesive side down on the fabric, and fuse it in place. The only drawback is that fusible web has a texture that may leave an impression in the foil.

   - *Liquid fusible web* lets you draw a design directly onto the fabric.

## DESIGNS

Freezer paper is very versatile for creating iron-on stencils. For a traditional stencil application, cut out a shape and use the empty space for adhesive application. Cut a positive image (or use the shape cut out when making a previous stencil) and apply the adhesive outside of the blocked space. For different effects, cut out the stencil with decorative scissors or tear the freezer paper to create a feathered-edge look.

### Positive or Negative?
Positive shapes are spaces in artwork that are filled with something, such as lines, designs, color, or shapes. Negative shapes are empty or void spaces, the space around an object or form; they're also called white space.

Masking tape also works for creating stencils. Use it in the same way as freezer paper to create positive and negative shapes.

Premade stencils are available at quilt, fabric, and craft stores. To use, position the stencil on the fabric and apply the adhesive in the area to be foiled with a brush or sponge. If the stencil is large, tape it to the fabric to prevent shifting.

Rubber stamps are another design source. Apply the adhesive to the stamp with an up-and-down motion. Place the stamp straight down on the fabric without rocking it and lift it straight off. Some adhesives will destroy rubber stamps, so be sure to wash the stamps immediately with soap and water.

## APPLYING FOIL WITH HEAT

1. Use an iron on the cotton setting to attach freezer paper to the fabric wrong side, or place the fabric on a piece of newspaper.

2. Apply adhesive to the fabric right side using the design and method you choose. Let the glue dry to a very lightly tacky state; a hair dryer may speed this process.

Apply the adhesive to the fabric.

3. On a firm ironing surface, carefully position the foil sheet with the shiny colored side up on the fabric, covering the applied adhesive. Set a dry iron to the wool setting (about 300° F).

4. Place a press cloth over the foil; ironing directly on the foil will damage both it and the adhesive. Iron the foil for 10 seconds using small, circular motions; make sure that all areas of the design come in contact with the heat.

5. For full coverage, allow the fabric to cool completely, and then gently peel away the plastic sheet. The foil will stick only to the areas where the adhesive was applied. For a lighter concentration of color, remove the foil while it's slightly warm.

Gently peel away the plastic film covering the foil.

6. In an area where the foil is sparse, a second color can be applied. The foil will adhere as long as there is glue still exposed and available. When applying one color of foil over another, lower the iron heat to a silk-nylon setting (approximately 225° F).

**Smaller Is Better**
For better control of the foiling process, work in one small area at a time.

## USING LIQUID FUSIBLE WEB

The heat application is very different with liquid fusible web than with other adhesive types.

1. While the fusible web is still wet, place the foil on the web, with the shiny, colored side up.

2. Cover with a press cloth and iron with a hot, dry iron for 20 to 30 seconds.

3. Let the fabric cool completely, and then peel off the plastic film. If less coverage works better for the design, remove the plastic film while the fabric is still warm from the iron.

## BURNISHING

Burnishing is a simple, hands-on way to apply foil with no heat source required.

1. Follow steps 1 and 2 of the heat-application method.

2. On a firm surface, carefully position the foil sheet with its shiny, colored side up on the fabric right side, covering the adhesive.

3. Rub the foil firmly using a wooden craft stick, a paperclip, a bone folder, or other burnishing tool to adhere the foil to the adhesive. This also separates the foil from its plastic covering.

Burnish the plastic-covered foil
to adhere it to the fabric.

4. Peel away the plastic sheet; the foil will stick only to the burnished areas where you applied the adhesive.

## CLEANING

1. To wash a garment embellished with foiling, turn it inside out and wash it by hand or machine using the gentlest setting. Use a mild detergent and no bleach.

2. Hang the garment or lay it flat to dry. Do not tumble dry or iron it.

3. Never dry-clean a foil image.